RIGHT HERE
RIGHT NOW
MEDITATIONS

Satsang Invitations for
Expanding Awareness, Volume I

Right Here, Right Now Meditations

Satsang Invitations for Expanding Awareness, Volume I

Canela Michelle Meyers

Third Edition Published in the United States, 2017; Second Edition Published in the United States, 2015; Electronic Edition Published in 2014; First Edition Published in Great Britain, 2011.

Sun-Eye Logo, Cover Painting, and Chapter Line Drawings: Canela Michelle Meyers
Author's Photos: Steve Clippingdale

Library of Congress Cataloging-in-Publication Data

Right Here, Right Now Meditations: Satsang Invitations for Expanding Awareness, Vol. 1
Canela Michelle Meyers

p. cm.
ISBN: 978-1-947708-00-6
Library of Congress Control Number: 2017957918
B19
10 9 8 7 6 5 4 3 2

CITRINE PUBLISHING

Asheville, North Carolina, USA
(828) 585-7030
www.CitrinePublishing.com

You are the Present.
The Gift of each moment.
You are the only one to receive
this gift, this Present;
Allow an unwrapping of That.

Will you relax enough to witness this unwrapping?
Thoughts, sensations, emotions, all that is revealed,
is simply the "wrapping paper" of the
Gift of Who you Are.

The invitation is:
to not get caught up in the wrapping paper,
to simply let it unfold to reveal
That which resides always;
The Truth of Who you Are.

∞ *Canela Michelle Meyers* ∞

This book is dedicated to my sons, Steven and Dani, for each showing me that we are all born innocent, whole, and completely unique.

Thank you for emanating these qualities so strongly and naturally that there is no room to doubt.

As I have said so many times, and say again here, I feel so grateful and honoured that you chose me as your mom!

Table of Contents

Acknowledgments

How to begin this part, who to acknowledge and where to begin when every single moment seems involved with all of the details and people in all that has been experienced? How to pull out the points that seem a bit bigger in absolutely everything? Wow, what a task, and here I go.

I am thankful to the Universe itself, which has given me the way that I am, the human being here and the experience of living as it has been, as it is and what comes next.

In the process of Realization, there is great thankfulness to Isaac Shapiro for his pointing to the Truth slightly prior to the moment when it was Realized. Thanks also to Paul Lowe for his support in pointing to the beauty of the human being; ways of relating in true intimacy; as well as his book *The Experiment is Over*, which stated that anyone could "wake-up." When I read that, at that moment, I felt the truth of it and it became a possibility for me.

My heart wishes to include those who are not in physical form any longer, yet have shown me such great loving, respect and support throughout my life so far: dear Osho, Papaji, Ramana Maharshi, Jesus, Quan Yen, Sri Ranjit, Ganeshaji, Kali Durga, Vishnu, and the all of the Angels, Fairies, and Animals who are with me in various moments, your presence keeps me humbly and joyfully crushed in heart.

Thankfulness is also felt toward my mom and dad for being exactly that: a mom and a dad to me and remaining in body long enough that I have had the honour of getting to know you as people, friends, and family.

I am thankful to so many people who have been supportive of this book coming into existence…here are a few of them:

- That it came into being now, rather than a few more years down the road, was directly supported by Doug Christou, who initiated, through a series of events, a date for the book to be finished by in 2011.

- Friends such as Nicole Deagan, Alison Cahill, Nancy Riecken, Saria Cundal, Donalda Meyers, and Alexandra Busse, who have been along with me in the making these Invitations into a book, holding a space with me when I have asked for it, and perhaps even when I didn't, as the steps that could happen, did. Extra thanks to Donalda for being such a great support in publishing the e-book.

- Wayne Froese for his support with the website, which has been such a blessing over the years—the website being an integral part of sharing the Invitations which ended up being in this book as well as the sharing that there is a book.

- Jane Covernton for her ever so valuable and just-right support as my editor.

- All of the people who have hosted Satsang with Canela gatherings starting in 1999 up until now—giving this Canela space to share and support others to remember what they know to be true. And, of course, all of the people who attended these Satsang gatherings! (That there were people who were interested in the Invitations supported them to be created).

- The other authors in author's circles, who collaborated with me in such mutual enjoyment, support, and practical application.

- Dani Riecken and Steve Clippingdale for listening to the Invitations prior to my sending them out to ensure that they made some sort of sense and extra thanks to Steve for his support in many ways while the book was coming into form.

- Steven Riecken for being able to translate a PDF file into a Word file when all of my electronic copies disappeared. This made the relaunching of this book possible!

Thank You!

Foreword

Canela has had the great fortune of recognising Truth. All Sages throughout time point at this, That in which the entire Universe, time, matter, and space appears.

Many stop here, thinking that they have arrived. However, in my view, this recognition begins a whole new level of an amazing process, where whatever has been unconscious starts to become conscious. I like to call this aspect of our journey: an exquisite love affair with all that is.

This process is a fire in which everything that your body/mind has worked diligently to try and protect and make sure never happens, starts to arise and can be extremely challenging. Once there is the recognition that this is Grace, then these experiences become opportunities and this fire keeps revealing its subtleties, which are infinite. One way of describing being available to this fire is service to all.

What becomes satisfying and fun in this love affair, is to be available to all beings, in the deep recognition that there is no separation, pointing out and inviting yourself in all the numerous forms to this incredible love affair.

This book is an expression of that fun. Savour it!

—Isaac Shapiro
    International Pointer at What's True
    Author of *Outbreak of Peace* and *It Happens by Itself*
    www.isaacshapiro.org

Introduction

The Invitations in this book first started to emerge in 2008. People who came to Individual Satsang sessions or ReiKi sessions with me often requested some follow-up written material on what came up in the time spent together, or to write down the steps that occurred—ones that I have found are repeated for many people, which they have found supportive, so are offered again and again.

Also, there were so many instances where people would share with me (outside of sessions or Satsang gatherings) what they were dealing with in their lives that I felt might be shifted by writing a little set of instructions of how to be with what was happening as energy. It seemed to me that people did not need to come to be with me in person for a session to support them, that they could support themselves if they only knew how.

After working with so many different people for over fifteen years by 2008, it was seen that these issues were often common ones and any "steps" that could be taken might be supportive to many people.

So the Invitations were written and sent out to everyone who was available via email and interested in receiving them. They were a way to offer support at no cost where people could help themselves in these common, human situations such as: conflict in the workplace or in their primary relationship; how to change patterns they seem stuck in; how to manifest more of what their hearts are calling for; how to move beyond lack, beyond survival into affluence; and for some, how to recognize doubt for what it is and to not get caught up in it as well as recognizing attachment to experiences—the attempt to get an experience to repeat itself—a common one for people whose interest has invited more and more "spiritual" or "cosmic" experiences.

The feedback received was that the Invitations were, in fact, supporting people to live more easily in their lives, more at ease with themselves and with whatever details happened to be happening in their lives. People said that they could return to the same Invitation at a later time and learn something new from it that they hadn't seen in the first reading. After a while, a number of different people suggested that the Invitations be made available in book form...and here you have it! This is the origin of how the Invitations came into being and the organic evolution of how you find this book in your hand today.

The intention of these Invitations is to support you, the reader, in living your life more peacefully, enjoyably, abundantly and fully. They are also intended as a support in allowing yourself to Realize the Awakened State of Being, expanding Awareness until that which is illusion is seen for what it is. The Invitations are only pointing to that which you already know—supporting you to remember, with the added touch of opportunities of being more loving toward yourself, and then, therefore, toward others.

There are quite a few books which speak of the Nothingness of Reality. This is true, Nothing is here. "No- thing" is another way to say something about nothing. Nothing reading words from Nothing in this moment ...and...we are also human.

There is an "expression": a happening within this Nothing. I call this the "humanness"—an expression of life itself, seen from a unique angle which is you your Self. This, to me is an expression of Love, this is how it is seen and felt, inside and out. For no reason whatsoever, the expression continues to occur and we get to Be With that expression as it is happening. This is the gift of life: we get to be aware of the occurrence of all that is, as it happens.

This book is in celebration of that—that *we are human* and that being human comes with opportunities (unique to each one) of being with the expression of Self more and more deeply. How can one possibly be with Nothing more and more? That is one of the most beautiful mysteries of life!

How to Make Best Use of These Invitations

Every Invitation in this book has been explored through direct experience by Canela herself, not just hearing about it from someone else. They are checked out, test driven, experienced.

These Invitations contain healing, supportive energy in the words, so regardless of whether they make cognitive sense (they are intended to make sense, but they might not) simply reading them can be supportive.

Read them softly, allowing the words to come to you rather than trying to "get" them, allowing the body and the mind to relax open to receive them. Then go a step further and explore what the Invitation actually invites. This can support you to allow shifts of energy (on all levels—mind, body, soul, energy field) towards greater awareness of this life that is being lived by you.

Reading one Invitation per week works well for many people. They have been likened to a "reading meditation"—like an eating meditation or walking meditation—inviting you to slow down enough to actually experience what is happening as you are reading. The Invitations often invite exactly that in the words, and certainly in the energy.

Allow yourself the time and space to be with each topic, to let it integrate with you, to explore it in whatever way it suggests or however it occurs to you to do so. Giving these topics some time to "cook" with you can support even more shifts towards awareness deepening. It is also how they actually evolved—they were written and sent out to people about a week before we would gather in person in Satsang where there would be a going over the Invitation and inviting a further deepening, understanding and opening with each person present as well as the group together. This process of the Invitation being written then sent out prior to Satsang gatherings is still in play as these words are written.

Sometimes the Invitations may not make sense at first, or seem confusing. These Invitations are not inviting the mind to engage itself over all else (the mind to dominate); they are inviting That which is beyond the mind (yet includes it) to be recognized, felt, and realized. They are pointers toward That which cannot be described, yet speaking about it through real happenings can help to magnify "it" so "it" is more obvious, more palatable. The suggestion to read one per week also gives this time or space for That Which Is, to touch its very own Self awake.

As with everything suggested in this book, this too is only an "invitation"—being with one per week is simply a suggestion. Reading them however it feels right to you is just great!

It has also been suggested that the book can be used in spontaneous support, allowing the book just to fall open to an Invitation. In other words, they do not need to be read in any particular order. They were not written in the order that you find them; they were later organized by topic to support the existence of a "table of contents" so you could have an idea of what's in this book.

At the beginning of each chapter, there is a little introduction to the chapter along with a simple line drawing symbolizing the chapter.

Capitalization of *That, Self,* and *Awareness*

As you may have noticed in the Introduction, sometimes the word "That" is capitalized. This is done when it is used to point to Consciousness* or Awareness itself. "That" always points to that which is directly occurring in each moment, the moment itself, which can only be pointed to because it cannot be described, only experienced. (Same thing for "Self" and "Awareness").

* Consciousness is:

●

Everything that is moving, everything that is still and that
● which is aware of this movement and stillness.
No less than everything in appearance, and also the space
● which everything appears in.
All that is seen, experienced, expressed in each moment—
Awareness itself; That which is Aware of its Self.

CHAPTER ONE

Loving Happening

Canela.

This chapter title says it all to me...that this is
what is happening here right now.
Yes, right here, right now,
loving is happening
in multitudes of expression.

You may notice that these words are speaking of a happening,
not that it happened, or will happen, it is happening.
Loving Happening.

Isn't it loving that the breath is just here,
being breathed; the blood just here, being pumped;
that the molecules that make up this "you"
continue to express themselves as "you"?

This is something to consider
about what is happening: is it seen as loving?
If it is, it will be experienced as loving.
It may not be how it is for everyone...it's just
what is being invited.
Look to see if it is
Loving in the moment...find out for yourself.

Living Without Demand on One's Self

Whan you feel like you *"have to"* do something, whatever that something is, I invite you to take a moment and feel into it to see if you really do. Stop the push of energy on yourself and really discern whether what you are about to push yourself to do, really does "have to" be done. Use the question: "will someone die if I didn't do this?" to support yourself to look at it realistically.

If it is something that you feel "has to" get done, then look for a way to do so without pushing yourself. See if you can find a way to follow through with whatever it is, without pushing yourself into it.

If you cannot find a way to let go of the push on yourself, *do not do it* and it will always work out for the better—every time. This takes trust. Very few people are living this way yet, and it is not always easy to do until you get the hang of it with practice.

To martyr one's self supposedly "for love" is not loving at all, and usually builds resentment. In other words, to push one's self over your own boundaries "because you feel you have to," because everyone else does, or you feel you "owe" someone, or for whatever reason, is coercing yourself. It has been a habit of our society to force one's self to do things against one's self. This then teaches (is modeled for) our children to do things against their own selves. This is not a natural way to live at all, nor does it support honesty. When you honestly do not want to do something, just be honest with yourself and don't do it. Trust yourself (which is also trusting Life itself) and see what happens.

To Choose Love or Fear

This week's invitation to yourself is to highlight apparent "Choice": choices to be made in each moment that they may come—to choose Love or Fear.

From the perspective of Awareness, the choices come and go in appearance and how you respond to them is actually choice-less—which one can see after it has occurred—you would've made that choice every time if the opportunity were to reoccur. However, in the same moment, they do appear to be choice points that you get to make and this is what is being pointed to here in this invitation.

Sometimes these choices may appear to be bigger choices as in choosing to let go of a relationship, and sometimes they might be smaller ones as in whether to have an ice cream sundae or a salad.

For each person, in each moment, the choice that feels more expansive and loving could be one or the other. The ice cream might be the choice or the salad, depending on the person choosing and what they feel in that moment. This is righteousness—what feels right and true in the moment...what feels more loving and inclusive? Or what feels like a pulling or push away; an exclusion; a making smaller; a withdrawing or neutral? Listen to what your heart feels.

It takes courage and experience to choose Love. Remember

an experience of when you have chosen fear—you can look back and see when those moments were. How did that choice serve you or others? What was your experience? Compare that with when you have chosen Love. It is in remembering those moments of choosing Love that you can support yourself to choose Love again, to gift yourself courage in the moment.

Love expands and supports everything; fear contracts or dominates and always costs someone—yourself.

This is all about connecting with yourself, with Love, and strengthening your experience of That...which in turn, supports you to choose Love over fear in any moment that you are asked by Life to choose.

Recognizing, Honouring, and Appreciating Your Self

This week's invitation is to play with acknowledging and appreciating yourself very directly on all levels. Most people have been taught to look outside of themselves to be recognized; to be heard; to be acknowledged; and to be appreciated.

This is a common mistake since, as with everything, both recognition and acknowledgement need to come from within you before they can flourish outside of you. In fact, you will likely not even hear or feel anything from any outside source until you have appreciated yourself. Or if you do feel something, it can be like a sugar rush leaving you wanting more and feeling unfulfilled and empty.

So, if you have found yourself continually let down because you've been looking for approval, appreciation, and/or acknowledgement from your parents, your partner, your children, or from anyone around you, the invitation is to stop, at long last, and give this to yourself.

Make a list of all of the things that you have brought yourself through, of all the times that there was concern or uncertainty as to whether you were going to make it or not. Perhaps it was a rough childhood that you made it through, perhaps the death of a parent at a young age, or an unstable marriage and then divorce…whatever it might be, please do take a few minutes and acknowledge yourself, appreciate yourself, honor yourself for having made it through those rough waters. However that was, you made it through to Now. Go and look directly into your own eyes in a mirror, relax your body, breathe deeply and speak your recognition to yourself.

Allow your words to sink into and merge with your body, mind, Being while you breathe deeply.

If you have been pining to be recognized for your brilliance, for your good work, for your good deeds, for your amazing talents, for your ability to enjoy life…well, it's time you simply gave that recognition to yourself. After all, you know what talents and abilities are with you. You are the one that has been with you in each and every moment. Be honest with yourself. Write yourself an email or a letter, phone yourself and leave a message on your own voicemail—let yourself hear what you need to hear.

The invitation is to stop and look at what you may have been attempting to get from others and to finally gift it directly to yourself. Appreciating yourself is very healing for you and everyone around you.

Acknowledging "Mother"

This invitation is for you to consider and acknowledge "Mother." Everyone came from the womb of some mother, grown in there in the perfect atmosphere—the perfect combo of food coming in, the perfect temperature, a double energy field protecting you (yours and your mother's), floating in fluid.

It's no wonder that "mother" is clung to so strongly perhaps as an attempt to return to that so totally supported world. The only mistake is that this longing to return gets attached to the person who is the mother—with all of the entitlement, expectations and therefore disappointments, of how it is "supposed to be or have been" in the idea of a "mother," looking for that all-giving support, that felt sense of safety and protection where all of your needs are met.

That feeling of having all of your needs met, as when you were carried in the womb, is available. It is available through opening to Consciousness, to allow the direct experience of all of your needs being met, letting go of the idea that your needs were ever not met; that you, as Awareness, can directly experience the incredible safety and security that is the Truth; that nothing whatsoever can remove this. It has been given and continues to be given long before the birth and long after the death of the human body.

Connect with That and relax into your experience of being human. Relax any ideas of the person who is your mother, or was your mother, no matter what she is like or has done, and tune into the True One—gifting yourself with the Love and Security that has always been yours. The only mistake was in looking for That outside of yourself. Instead allow the felt sense of that inside, which encompasses the outside.

You could also acknowledge the person who is your mother, that she carried you and gave birth to you, that somewhere along the line there was a deal made between your souls to be in this life together. Like the sure things in life, you cannot change who your mother is. It has already happened. She will always be your mother as a human even if you don't know who she is.

Then, after this birth, there may have been a mother, your blood mother or adopted mother perhaps, who took care of you as a vulnerable newborn, a young child, a teenager, who may even be still supporting you in some ways now, whether in body or after her death. Her Love is with you…acknowledge this too.

And if you're a mother, tending to the needs of your children, whether young or grown, acknowledge this aspect of yourself and all of your experiencing and sharing in that.

For myself, the Mother is the Absolute, holding me, embracing me, inside and out. She holds all of creation, supporting it to express itself however it does.

And, there is a woman who is my mother, who gave birth to me some time ago and who is still in body. In celebrating her, instantly I am also celebrating the fact that I exist as a human being—as Awareness traipsing around with this body, mind, soul: this expression of One that I get to tend to and experience life through and with.

Being also a mother myself, what a great honour it has been and is, to be with these two Beings who chose me as a mom and who have taught me so very much! For my own mother, and myself as a mother I am profoundly grateful…wow! What a gift!

There is also a gratefulness, so deeply, to Consciousness; to the Absolute for this Awareness that knows its Self. This is really a crazy thing, because it is towards one's Self that one is grateful…something Being so very thankful to Be itself and yet it continues to happen: this thankfulness. It celebrates itself and includes every bit of the humanness happening…what a most incredible blessing!

Catch 22

This invitation to see and experience the "Catch 22" in Love. For those that may not be familiar with the expression "Catch 22," it can be a term that is sometimes used to define a situation that goes round and round—the ending flows back into the beginning, creating a loop that goes on and on.

So this "Catch 22" of Love?

When you allow yourself to experience the Love that exists in each moment, no matter what the details are, you cannot help but also see that you are not alone—that the Universe is conspiring (and has been conspiring all along) to support you in each moment, and "knows" exactly how to support you.

As one recognizes this support—recognizes direct examples from their own life—there is a further relaxing open, a greater Trust emerges, and then in turn, more experiencing life as a loving experience, an experience of Being Loved. There's the loop…on-going and also deepening at the same time as it is expanding. This would be a purposeful "Catch 22," a loop that you want to be caught in rather than one you are stuck in.

Opening to Love, allows support; recognizing support, deepens Trust; more Trust, more opening to Love and so on, and so on.

Expanding Love

Love is an experience, often mixed up with details that appear outside of one's self, as if it were reliant on that, but thankfully, it is not. Love is something that happens inside, perhaps invited by something, someone or a scene of beauty perhaps—and Love is felt—you feel it within yourself.

When we spend time even musing about Love, Love is expanded. So this is what is occurring right now as you read this!

A great way to support Love in your life experience is to go to the mirror, look into your own eyes, breathe deeply, relax and stay a few moments relaxing with yourself like this.

Who is this wonderful person looking with you? Can you feel your heart melt open. Perhaps there is a soft smile, or are you uncomfortable and not wanting to look? This is just information for you, nothing "wrong" or "right" about what happens. Play with this some more; if there is discomfort, give yourself some space, some time to relax towards yourself while you feel the energy of discomfort, Being with That as it is with you. Feel your heart as you look, letting go of any judgements that might rise, rest, relax and Be With you while being in contact with your heart. See what happens with the energy that looked like discomfort at first.

Love is an experience, one that you already know when it is happening. You can invite new experiences of Love or a deepening into Love as you rise in the morning, or as you are going to sleep at night (anytime works too!) by simply saying either out loud or silently to yourself: "I invite more experiences of Love into my life now." Or use words that are yours if you wish, whatever feels the most right is right for you. Once you have stated it, let it go and see what happens.

Experiences of Love, here in this invitation, mean exactly that: it may be that a person will come into your life and your heart will flutter; it may be that in meditation Love will come and take you in its embrace; it may be some sort of invitation that at first may not look like Love; or you may feel whole new levels of Love with your mother, father, sister, or brother, dog, cat, home, etc. It can show up as Joy, Contentment, and/or Gratitude—all wonderful flavours of Love. Do you really know, realize, or feel how Loved you are?

Open to being shown Love newly—Love itself is just waiting for the invitation! Yes, deliberately commit yourself to opening to an even greater experiencing of Love, even more directly, even more fully…to allow the felt sense of Love to expand.

CHAPTER TWO

Trusting Every Aspect

Canelo.

What is meant here by "trust"?

*The trust of a child, who wobbles forward toward you as
you hold out your hands…this is a vision of it.*

*If you spend a moment now, remembering moments of
trust that you have experienced,
you might notice that there was
a felt sense of some part of you opening
toward whatever the details are. To trust is to open
yourself towards what is.*

*Sometimes trust is unconscious…like the trust
that is with you when you are walking
and go to put your foot down—that there will be some
ground for it to land on.
Or that when you go to sleep at night, you will wake up
the next morning…that the next morning
comes and here you are.*

Impermanence

This week's invitation is to play with, and experience directly, the reality of impermanence. To invite you to experience impermanence directly is kind of funny as you are experiencing that in each moment whether you're aware of it or not. The invitation is to realize that which is occurring—that no matter what it is that you are experiencing (other than Awareness itself), it is not permanent…the experience will change.

This then, can be such a soothing realization. If one is experiencing fear, one can relax open and be aware of the fear, feel it and watch it change. The only thing that keeps an experience happening is if you feed it or try to get rid of it.

Say, for example, the fear of mortal death arises. One's mind may come up with all sorts of reasons why the fear of death is relevant to you, that with all of this evidence, you "should" be feeling fear of death. After all, you can look to your past experience and justify feeling the fear—yes?

When in actuality, if you look and are honest with yourself, even the fear of death comes and goes. For instance, if you are lying down on the couch watching TV, the fear may not be present. If you were then to look for your fear, your very looking can actually activate it.

That mortal death will come is true. One way or another, it

will come to each and every human. If fear of death is present then, use your knowledge of impermanence and relax open to feeling the fear until it passes. After all, fearing death will not change that mortal death will come, while staying with the fear and feeding it (instead of feeling it) can actually magnetize death closer. If it is time, then it is time.

The same then, holds true for any experience. You can look to your own experiencing to validate this truth. In the past, there may have been moments of extreme cold or physical discomfort—moments where one could imagine that you would never forget such pain, like childbirth, and yet forgetting happens as one experiencing follows another and another and so it goes.

This knowledge of impermanence can support a relaxing, a freedom, a trust, to allow yourself to feel whatever it is that is occurring; to relax open to it; Be With That; and it will change right before the Awareness that you are.

A Deal With Your Self

This week's invitation is to play with making a deal with your Self: to commit to making Consciousness your priority and asking your Self to support your Self to That in each moment—whatever it takes, unconditionally.

With a commitment, sincerely given to yourself, the moment of choice may just ring a little more loudly, more obviously when it happens. That there IS a choice will become more bold face. Somehow, such a commitment enlivens those moments where a shift can occur.

You can also lean back on your commitment and let it support you through whatever you need to be with in order to come to your new and more fulfilled way of Being, reminding yourself in the moment, that as scary as that new step may feel, or as uncomfortable as you might be in the midst of change, you asked for it—from your Self to your Self by this commitment—and who better to trust than your Self?

Harmony—Inviting This Within and Without

Whether we are aware of it or not, nature is always looking to bring balance to itself. This happens within and without—within: in the divine masculine and feminine parts of yourself, the yin and yang, the dark and the light; without: as all of this which appears to be outside of yourself.

Nothing is "bad" or "wrong." Only perhaps, in some moments, there is an imbalance. The universe will collaborate to bring balance to whatever is out of balance. If you allow a space to see this balancing act from your own experience, you will see that this has been happening all along.

What this balancing is also called is: Healing. Healing yourself to wholeness. That sounds as if "you" are doing something, when really it is an allowing happening. Your very nature will attempt to bring harmony or balance in every moment. When imbalance is happening, we can see and feel it in the discomfort that it may bring. That is all that the discomfort is attempting to show us, that something is out of balance. Looking at life and its happenings from this perspective makes it all easier discomfort becomes an indicator rather than something to get rid of as harmony is being invited directly when discomfort is present.

Satsang supports this way of harmony—one can give harmony itself space to come into itself. Discomfort can lead the way (by feeling it fully) to harmony and then this is the experience of Peace with All.

Happening Too

This week's invitation is one that invites you to take up Dr. Seuss's offer:

"Out there things can happen and frequently do,
to people as brainy and footsy as you.
And when things start to happen,
don't worry, don't stew,
just go right along,
you'll start happening too!"

From *The Places You'll Go* by Dr. Seuss

When "things" start to happen, whatever those "things" are, open up to them instead of closing down or attempting to change them. Yes, open to them and just see what happens when you do.

This is an invitation to deepen your commitment to your Self to be able to open to whatever it is that is happening; to see/feel what it truly is and to let it Be; to accept That.

As an example: your mother, sister or brother comes running into the room, all upset about something, yelling loudly perhaps. The automatic response might be to attempt to "fix" whatever it is they are yelling about, or defend yourself if it is some sort of attack on you for something you did. Instead, when things start to happen (just like this), see what happens if you breathe, be still, and open up your body, relax yourself open, feel yourself and what is happening, and then respond. This can be done with your eyes open or closed, whichever is best for you. Let whatever it is that is happening "come in" first, by relaxing your body, your system open, relaxing the contraction. Give it some space, and then respond however it feels appropriate to do so in that moment…go along with the happening instead of attempting to stop it, change it or withdraw from it.

Trust

This invitation is the biggie, the one that if you decide to take it, will turn your life around: Trust yourself. Open up to trusting what your own heart says, no matter what you might imagine the consequences may be. The heart does not think, it Knows. In a world made up of nothing but Love Consciousness, your heart is your leader. It will get you into situations in which you get to explore your way to balance. And the side effect is cleansing and embodiment that could happen in no other way.

Trusting others can only be limited because you are not them and have not lived the moments that they have lived. So although something may be totally in alignment, in integrity for them, it may look totally untrustworthy to another.

What you can Trust, if you feel to trust another is: in that moment, check out what your heart says...if "yes," then it is you, trusting yourself to trust—that's how you can include the other in your Trust.

The only one to Trust, the only one you truly have access to, in each and every moment, is yourself. And, the only way to gain Trust in yourself, is to Trust yourself! Take the steps in whatever direction your heart knows is true, then you will receive the real results, the real response of the Universe to Trust, and therefore, Trust yourself even more.

Can you let go to That? Can you hear and act on what you know is true from your heart? You are the only one who can answer that.

Your heart is only attempting to Love you, always, all ways.

CHAPTER THREE

Relating for Real

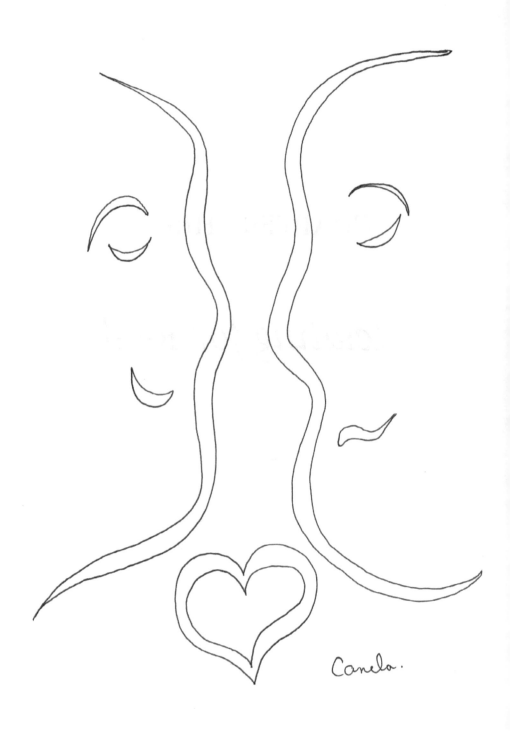

Canela.

Relating for real is a chapter of invitations
that invite you to look at
how you might relate with your world,
and with others.

Not just relating as if one were
a player in a story—acting out
one's part as best as
one imagines they are supposed to.

For this book,
it is inviting one to look at
what exactly is really happening
in the moments of relating—what is really going on
when you stop and take a moment to explore?

Relating vs. Relationship

The invitation here is to acknowledge that how it is you relate to the world in all its facets—with people, with yourself, with your home, with issues—it is a happening, not a stagnant "thing"…it is an in-the-moment relating.

Using the word "relating" is far more true than using the word "relationship." Relationship speaks about a "ship" or container of something and so leads one to describe it as if the way of it is the same in each moment when this cannot be true.

For example, how is your relationship with your mom? What a very vast question—the only response can be: when are you asking about? How "is" my relating with my mom now? In the moment of asking, I can tune in and feel that, respond with the information that rises in response. Truly, it is a "relating"…it is something that is moving and changing in each moment.

How "was" the relationship with my mom? Again, there are so many variations; there is a need for a "when" to answer this question. Generalizing over a lifetime about such a thing really doesn't do the relating any kind of justice nor is it very real. There can be a perception of how it was and this perception is right in the moment of looking.

How is your relationship with yourself? Even asking the question makes one attempt to define this as a thing, rather than a happening. How is your relating with yourself right now? This invites one to look right in the moment of the asking—this is where reality rests, in each moment.

Conflict or Opportunity?

This week, the invitation is to support you to explore the possibility of each and every conflict as an opportunity. When there is an apparent "conflict," look to see what is really going on by stopping in the midst of the conflictive energy that is happening and that you are likely feeling.

Once stopped by your own curiosity, open your body, breathe, and feel where the energy is "speaking" something inside of yourself. It might feel heavy, constricted or agitated in one area (or all) of your body—just look for whatever stands out in that moment, breathe, relax open, and feel it, watch the energy move, let it reveal itself to you, relaxing all of the rest of your body even more, so it has more space to be.

If the conflict is between two people, both parties will have something to explore if both people feel the conflict. If one person stops, looks within, feels what is going on (and therefore embraces whatever the conflict is supporting to be seen/felt in that moment) it does not mean that the conflict is her or his "fault." There will usually be two sides to every conflict if there are two people involved (more people involved = more opportunities).

Usually, when a person opens up to what is really happening —feeling the energy inside of themselves in the moment, witnessing that, as they relax open—whatever is experienced will be very different from the energy of the conflict itself or the details that the conflict looked to be about.

If you've *not* been stopping to check out what is happening, and just let the "apparent other" (other person) find what it is about for them, then you are totally missing out on the opportunity.

To imagine that it is only about the other person simply because they happened to have found the underlying energy, is a cop out towards yourself. It may seem that the whole thing happened just for the other to find some bit of life to admit, to embrace, and you might use that as some sort of defense to then say to yourself, "See, it was all about them, therefore I am 'right' and therefore I will not explore it." This would be defending the very part of you that stands in your own way of your Self.

The Self, Awareness, as you, is constantly inviting an embracing, an embodiment of the human aspect as a reflection or display of itself. Awareness is constantly, in each moment, revealing its Self to its Self—and this is the opportunity that you might be passing over, again and again, avoiding your very Self by imagining it isn't about you.

To admit the Truth of what is really happening is to embrace one's self…as humbling and vulnerable as it might feel in a moment. You are invited to explore this directly, supporting your Self to move more and more fully to the Truth of What Is.

Allowing Perception of "The Truth"

This week's invitation is to invite you to play directly with your own perception in each moment. Allowing yourself to see The Truth; hear The Truth, feel The Truth, open fully to The Truth, Be The Truth and everything that is experienced will actually be The Truth. This is not an invitation to "think" about what it is that is being invited here, it can only be "experienced" through allowing it, by trying it out, playing with it.

For example: in any moment, there might be people arguing right there with you, or it may even be yourself in the argument. In that very moment, register in your mind: "This is the Truth," open your body, mind, and energy field and be present to what is.

It is not about judging whatever is happening—by asking questions like: is it "about the Truth" or not? Is it good or bad? Just open to whatever is actually happening right as soon as you remember to do so, and experience what happens. Once the mind reminds (re-minds) you to open yourself up to What Is, let go and receive all of the information that is happening right in that moment—inside and out. When you are in "receiving" mode (open to experience whatever is) judging ceases to exist.

Then, as an example, it becomes: The Truth speaking, The Truth yelling, The Truth smiling, The Truth hearing, The Truth smelling. The Truth is whatever is happening in the moment of the experiencing…including yourself. Consciously opening to That magnifies it and makes it easier to see and experience directly.

Communication

This week's invitation is to play with communication with yourself and also with others. When you read that: "communicating with yourself," there is this idea that you know what is meant by that…without thinking about it, that you know what is meant.

Taking a closer look, when you do communicate with yourself and it seems like a two-way thing, what are the two parts that are communicating? As an example, you might say to yourself inside, "Ok, time to go out to the garden" and you may hear your voice inside respond with, "Oh wait, phone your sister first" (really regular stuff). Actually look in that moment for those two players as they are present, to experience where and what they exactly are. You can hear the voice inside—where is it actually coming from?

This is not being suggested as something to "think" about; it is inviting that you look to see: who is it in that moment? And who is it that answers? Who is that really? Who is it that is looking for where the voice comes from?

Another way is also to look inside whenever you are communicating with another person. Directly in the moment, see who it is that is communicating—where does this "you" part come from? Again, not an answer from the mind, but an actual exploration to see where, in the moment, the part of you

that communicates with another, actually is and who is that?
Check it out.

Being Your Own Best Friend in Action—Not Just Thinking About It

Who is there (here) with you in every moment? You are. If there is a looking to fulfill an aspect of your life from outside of yourself, any grasping for that, whatever it is, be it Respect, Love, Attention, Interest, Nurturing, Security...be creative in the moment and give whatever it is to yourself.

Whenever there is disappointment, this is only an indicator that there is an expectation of something. Find the "something" and give it to yourself. Care enough for yourself to consider allowing what you would love for others, to give that to yourself. Realize whatever that is, in the moment of arising, and give it to yourself—somehow, someway, be creative, have fun, and find a way. Not as an act of independence, instead as an act of Being Loving toward yourself. Your way is the right way for you.

Explore this aspect of living and loving...you are welcome!

All is New

This invitation is to play with recognizing the newness of all that is. Everything is changing, is in movement, nothing remains the same. We all know this and have heard it perhaps many times. How can we apply this knowledge? By acknowledging the newness of all that one is aware of in each moment.

When you are chopping up veggies for supper, for example, watch those hands there, working with the vegetables, look at them as if you do not recognize them, watch them magically chop and handle, let go of any idea that you 'know' them, remember that they are new and open to that newness just to see what happens.

This is a great exercise to use with someone that you "think" you know. When next you meet, remember that they are new and open to that newness. You might find that thoughts may rise like: "Oh, I know him, he is the same"…let such thoughts come and go, remain open to the person as if they were new to you, as if you are meeting them for the very first time, allowing the curiosity that comes with meeting someone new.

This can be used in a multitude of ways—meet your shoes newly, feel your body newly, meet your pet newly, meet an apple or a plant newly, hear sounds newly—with open curiosity and see what happens. Even as you read this, see if you can drop your "knowing" of the computer or page you are reading and let it appear in its newness…let what you think you knew be new!

CHAPTER FOUR

Blame to Bliss

Wouldn't any movement that allows the energy of "blame"
to melt away be blissful?

Being in the energy of "blame"
is not a very comfortable experience, one that serves nothing,
except perhaps it may serve some sort of attachment
to being "right" because blame always says
something or someone is "wrong."
It is not a healthy stance to take,
no matter how "right" you think you are,
it is not an open or loving way to live.

It does not mean to bow down to unfair treatment,
unfair happenings do happen in life,
it is more of a matter of
how are you with this unfairness?

It would be blissful to be living without blame
and this is what this chapter is about—
inviting you to more of that.

Letting Go of Victimhood

This week's invitation is to look at, and be with, letting go of any energy related to being a victim. How to allow this? First off, let's define what "victimhood" energy is as it pertains to this invitation: it is any kind of energy (including ideas) that keeps you from moving in any direction because of fear of something that had happened in the past (that seemed against you) repeating itself.

Often it is not entirely known to what degree a person is holding fear around repetition of being a victim. What can be noticed is where a person seems unable to move forward in their relating with another or in their work, or to engage more deeply in life.

Most everyone has had some sort of happening where they ended up being a victim, where they themselves were taken advantage of by another, trespassed against in some way. Because this is a vast topic, especially because people often trespass against themselves, for this invitation, it is only in regards to happenings where another has apparently taken advantage of you, or something "unfair" has happened to you, or is happening currently.

When such happenings happened when you were a child, the energy is often held inside because to process and integrate the energy is just not possible for a child. The energy waits until you are able to be with it Consciously...to be with it responsibly in a time of your life that you understand what you are doing. Current happenings around victimhood are often linked to childhood experiences that you may not even be aware of.

Fighting for something more fair to happen will not integrate the energy and only emphasizes "againstness" in that something is held as "wrong"—which perpetuates the situation. The truth is: it has already happened, it has already been affecting you for however long it has—it cannot be undone once it has occurred. The energy that resulted because of it, however, can be unravelled to freedom.

This is how you can support that freedom: consciously allow the felt sense of being a victim to rise purposely, to give it space for it to be felt completely, then let the energy finish its process of unfolding so it no longer is held in your own way.

Steps to allow this:

- Create a safe place—either at home or with someone who understands what you are about to explore. Remember, this energy is already with you, it cannot overtake you, you are simply allowing it to move to its completion.

- Allow yourself to relax open, breathe deeply, and feel the chair (or whatever you are sitting or lying on). Remind yourself that you are safe, you are an adult, and you are ready to feel the energy within.

- Once you are relaxed, bring up the memory (either from the past or a current situation where you feel to be a victim). Allowing the memory to rise in the moment brings it present with you. Allow thoughts of remembering whatever the incidence was/is, then allow your attention to be aware of where these thoughts have an effect in your body.

- Feel that effect in your body, feel the energy moving or staying still or whatever it is that you feel. Be With That, while staying present to the fact that you are safe, in your home, and Consciously exploring this. Tune into the felt sense of your weight on the chair, relax your body to allow the energy to move as freely as possible. Let the energy unwind while you experience it.

- When it seems to be finished, bring up the memory of the happening again, and again let your attention be with the body to see if the effect is the same, different, or there at all. Repeat this until it feels complete.

This is a process of being responsible with What Is. Explore this further whenever it feels appropriate so you are more free to move with what your heart wants—letting go of energies that have been in your way up until now, by feeling them.

Being Responsible About It All

This invitation is to look at, and practice, responsibility. If there is any discomfort in your life, longstanding or in moments, and you think you have anyone or anything to blame for it, you are not being responsible.

The invitation here is to be very honest with yourself—are you "blaming" at all in any aspect of your life? I.e.: "Life would be great if only she/he were different"; "If only I could win a lottery, then life would be great!"; "If I **had** parents like hers, then I could do what I want too."

Are you blaming anything or anyone (including what you don't have) as a reason for not living your life more fully?

If so, then take some time to look inside, to invite yourself to let go of whatever is in the way of what you would like in your life—it will be inside of you if it shows up, in appearance, outside of you.

Let blaming be your indicator to look inside and let go of whatever you yourself are holding in the way of your own simple, joyful, abundant way of being. Not with your mind, thinking it over; instead feeling the energy inside of you, witnessing it as it moves, is how to "let go" of it. The letting go is actually a side effect of feeling the energy directly. Allowing yourself to experience it is the letting go…it moves itself.

Whose Power is It?

This week's invitation is to embrace your own "Power." It is rather odd to call it "yours" as really it belongs to Source like all else. And, you were given this life to tend to, to learn in, to learn mastery with everything, and to enjoy and relax into That.

So this idea of "yours" is really what you are responsible for—what you were given to take care of, or tend to in each moment, you this human who is experiencing life.

This responsibility of your power, then, is about wherever you may be giving your attention away—to others, to situations, to apparent past happenings, to apparent future happenings. Like scenarios where you feel something or someone is to blame or anything that appears to have any power over you.

There is a choice, once you find out what you have been up to, to stop giving your power away—no matter how "wrong" or how "unfair" the other person or life seems to be. It can be anything that may be repeating in your life, or people that you spend a lot of time thinking negative thoughts about.

Stop, breathe, relax open your body, relax open every molecule and call your energy back home to you from whatever, or whoever, seems to affect you in attracting your attention again and again. Draw "your" attention into the center of your body, your core, by being open there and allowing the energy in.

59

In reality, there is no one or nothing outside of yourself, so empower this One that you are instead of pilfering your energy away in a habit. After the movement of energy seems complete, allow your body to be as open as you can, let the energy of the other person, or situation, be released back to them. Whatever that might be, the energy itself will know, all you need do is just say it, think it—that so and so's energy be returned to them in support of them.

This is really a meditation and is all about supporting you home to yourSelf—to experience This That You Are. It is a meditation for letting go of any hindrances to that, and claiming your attention and energy to be able to use it for the good of all, including yourself.

Resolving Conflict Through Sharing

This is all about exploring resolving conflict through a sharing method, quite different than resolving apparent conflict through personal introspective, which is spoken of in another invitation in this book: "Conflict or Opportunity?"

That 'conflict' is not wanted is very handy as it makes it show up on the screen of your awareness more boldface or highlighted.

Over the years of working with people, families, and business situations, the same set of steps have worked to resolve conflict in each and every case. Not only is the conflict resolved, there have always been added benefit to the participants who are willing to explore conflict in this way. Rather than attempting to convince the other that you are "right" and they are "wrong" (with the other person attempting the exact same thing) why not give this some space to explore? Here are the steps:

- All parties involved in the conflict need to be interested in, and committed to, a win/win outcome to the situation.

- It is best to have a moderator—someone who is not involved in the conflict directly, to moderate these simple set of "rules" that all parties agree to prior to opening up the floor to the conflict itself.

- Each person is given the space to share what the conflict is from their perspective; the other(s) may not interrupt.

- Each person agrees to be as truthful as they can be.

- In the sharing time, the person shares the issue and how they feel about it—how they feel in response to this actual situation.

- Give this a time limit, with more time for more complex issues. Not more than fifteen minutes per person, unless there are only two people involved. You will find that if everyone is listening, each person will not need as much time.

- If you are doing this without a moderator, it is helpful to use something as a "talking stick"—it could be a spoon, or pen, anything like that. Of course this can be included even if there is a moderator, as it helps to make it clear whose turn it is. The person with the "stick" is the only person who can speak, except for the moderator if there is one.

- The moderator simply reminds people that they agreed not to interrupt if interruption happens. The moderator also supports the speaker to share feelings from "I feel," and keeps it to feelings, not judgements. For example, "I feel that he is a jerk" is not a feeling; it's a judgement.

- Every time that this method has been used to support conflict resolution, the conflict has been resolved. The people themselves figure out what steps need to be taken, if any, at the end of the session. Feedback has been, consistently, that they feel more at ease and connected with each other after exploring the conflict so directly. What a win/win for a relating, a family, or a business!

CHAPTER FIVE

Experiencing No-Separation/Oneness

Conela.

Chances are that you have heard of this Oneness—
this possibility of being aware
of living as One.

Many people have lots of ideas about what
this means when really, it is something
that a person can experience.
It is not something that the mind can grasp
except the mind can be cognizant in the experience of it.

The beauty of this living in No-Separation,
or as One, is that it is what is true already.
This idea that we are not all one,
or that there is separation, is only an idea
that is dispelled when the experience of
no-separation is happening.

These next invitations are in support of you
experiencing just this:
Oneness or No-Separation.
Experiencing Reality as it truly is.

What You Commit To

This week's invitation is to look at what the opportunity is around the money that flows your way, which in turn, you get to redirect to whatever you are committed to.

It is a commitment that you make when you exchange that paper stuff we call money (in whatever form you use—be it paper, coin, debit, or credit card) for an apple, for example. What is actually in that exchange?

A commitment to care for yourself by feeding yourself—this touches the apple and you. And it also touches the person who sold it to you, the person who packed it for delivery to the store, the driver who delivered it, the farm owner and workers, the tree the apple came from, the sun, rain, and earth that support the tree to be alive, the oxygen that the tree exhales helping to clean our environment, and all of the connections from each of those that branch out to eventually include absolutely everything and everyone that is.

When you put the money into the box for Satsang then, what is it you are committing to? The space of Satsang is for supporting everyone to embrace themselves unconditionally more and more; it is a very direct commitment to yourself. To support people to awaken to themselves—to all that is, to directly experience no-separation is what that space invites. It is simply a direct route, taken consciously when you understand this.

So this invitation is for you to consider what you are actually paying for when you pay for things. Follow the route of what you are affecting by your payment…you will find that it is always you that you are supporting, you yourself…it just happens to include a multitude of steps along the way, or a few steps (yet inclusive of all that is) as in the case of Satsang.

The Benefit of Discomfort or Uncertainty

This week's invitation is to look at, and be with, the benefit of discomfort or uncertainty. A very natural part of the awakening process can be strong discomfort or uncertainty—that's why not everyone is living in the awakened state (yet!)

Of course it might feel uncomfortable to come to a Satsang Meditation gathering, for example, and feel and experience things that you may not be able to label in any way or know, from your mind, what is happening. This can be quite scary for some people…of course it might be!

In the space of Satsang, there is support for that which is held to just melt away. Whatever the mind might be holding as a structure to make sense of the experience of being human, might dissolve. This is the very point that can be allowed—that that very discomfort is, in fact, your next step to open to, to be with, to relax as much as possible in the discomfort and discover what happens next.

The mind makes constructs out of outside details to create an illusion of reality. When that construct is shaken or dissolved, the person is left with absolutely nothing that the mind can attach to, to comfort itself. This is Reality—when there is nothing except for the current details happening that registers in the being, including the mind. This is totally different in each moment and unknown. This is why the Stateless State is an invitation to total trust in something bigger (Awareness) than how the world appears to be to the mind. To trust your direct experience—even though it has no structure, nothing to point to, nothing except the fact that something is experiencing something—to trust this real experience, allowing yourself to feel the discomfort (if it is there) until it too dissolves, this is the invitation from you yourself to you yourself.

This dissolving can occur within the experiencing of a Satsang gathering, it is exactly what the container of Satsang is for…that this can be experienced—you can speak of it, point to it, (in the moment) and Be With others who are experiencing it simultaneously which can be comforting to know that this Nothingness, this Emptiness, this direct dance of all dimensions, is an ok "place" to be as it is shared and experienced together.

So the benefit of the discomfort is that it can be an indicator that you are allowing more of yourself To Be—allowing yourself to experience That which is real without the construct. The very existence of the discomfort can actually become a comfort in that you are ready to Be—just as you are, no more, no less, exactly That.

Why Meditate?

This invitation is to look at, and be with newly, one of the main purposes of meditation. First, there is a need to clarify what is meant here by "meditation" as this word is used for many techniques of meditation. In this case though, it means the direct experiencing of "What Is."

What I mean by that is: not focussing on a mantra, not swishing your attention through your body, not praying to an image or idea of a higher being, not applying any known technique of meditation. These techniques have wonderful benefits, it is just not what is being pointed to here, now.

Meditation in this invitation is simply turning your attention inward, allowing information that may appear to be outside of yourself to come in. If you are sitting down and being still, closing your eyes is helpful if it makes it easier for you to allow awareness to rest inwardly as having your eyes open can engage a habit of your attention being with what you see outside of your system. If you are being active, while simultaneously being aware of what is happening inside, then closing your eyes may not be a good idea.

We are all born whole, innocent, and completely awake (we just aren't aware of that). Next comes a process that most of us are taught directly (and is modelled by almost everyone around us) of focussing our attention on objects and situations outside of ourselves, learning about a world made up of "things." This is not wrong it is just how our world is. And we need this, actually, so that we can tell the difference of when the awakened state, the stateless state, occurs. How could we know what Being Conscious is if we didn't have something to compare it to?

So, we were taught to have our attention "outward bound." Meditation, is resting with your attention inwardly: letting the sounds of outside happenings come 'in' to you, rather than your attention going 'out' to wherever the sound seems to be coming from; letting yourself feel any emotions or sensations that might be present, giving them space to be; allowing thoughts to come and go, noticing when you engage in them and responding to that engagement by bringing your attention newly to what is actually occurring in the moment—like feeling the weight of your body on the chair. Simply notice what is actually happening in the moments that you sit there quietly with yourself.

At first this type of meditation might not seem so dramatic as letting your attention run with the outside details, yet if you allow yourself space to settle into this, to come to a resting place within, after a while of practicing this, a balance begins to happen between that which appears outside and that which appears within, and the two come closer together. In other words, there will be less separation between yourself and that which appears to be outside of you.

In a Satsang gathering, it is easier to let go of the outside details when everyone present is going in the same direction—allowing themselves to drop into the inner realms…where the outside is not excluded, it just shows up on its own. Support yourself to more balance, peace, and awareness in your life through in the moment experiencing of yourself in meditation.

Letting Go of Needing to Know

T he topic of this invitation: letting go of needing to know, enticing the freedom of not knowing. When you think you know something, it totally limits what life would like to show you, to reveal to you. Nothing new can come into a space that thinks it already knows.

There is always more to experience no matter how much you "know" about life, about Consciousness. After all, when you experience full "Oneness" and realize that you do not actually exist (that you are in fact, nothing) how far can knowing something go in that?

Allowing yourself the space to "not know" creates an empty space where life can flow in to you. Yes, it may feel quite humbling and vulnerable since we are taught that knowing something is valuable and so are more comfortable with being filled up with information rather than emptiness. Then people compete for who knows more information and the one who knows more is smarter than the others. Really, it is not so smart, certainly not energetically.

Allow the nothingness of life, knowing nothing, to be with you. Being simply yourself as a human being, experiencing each moment without knowing what comes next. Living in that state of openness, a state of innocence and naturalness, allows life to support you more fully to more of What Is.

In not knowing, support is available in each and every moment, empowering you to live more easily, enjoyably, and harmoniously in every aspect of your experiencing. This is something to explore so you can find out the truth of it from your own direct experience.

CHAPTER SIX

Living Life by Feel – Emotional Intelligence

Ah, what a catchy chapter name;
Emotional Intelligence is such the rave these days. It has become
a great topic in the business world as coaches everywhere are
beginning to understand the relevance of what we feel to be of
great worth. This is a very straightforward concept when one
acknowledges that all is energy—
that every bit of this Universe is made of energy.

When such energies as emotions are present, they can tend to blot
out much of existence, that whatever emotion is being felt, it will
have all of our attention...especially emotions such as
grief, anger, and irritation.

Emotional intelligence simply turns around and looks at it like
this: ok, these emotions are here, what is it that they are
attempting to tell us by their "shouting," by the strength
of their existence?

The intelligence comes in by not looking at the emotion and
attempting to reason it out—why is it here? Or how can I
change it? Instead, intelligence invites us to feel our way with the
emotion...let it express itself to us and its mystery will unfold in
the acceptance of it. Feeling it is the same thing as accepting it
or embracing it.

How is this intelligent? Try it out and see for yourself. Any other
way of being with emotions when they rise can seem rather lame
once you experience this living life by feel. The next step can be to
apply the energy of the emotion in alchemy...but that's another
chapter to come.

Invitations to You Happening in Each Moment

This week's invitation is to look at what is happening, in any moment, as an invitation to be present. No matter what is happening, the moment itself will be full of reminders to support you to even more Presence…just look for them!

Even in the midst of some sort of uncomfortable kerfuffle—perhaps an argument with someone—stop in the middle of the happening and take a closer look. Feel whatever you are feeling, breathe deeply, let go of the details dancing on the surface, look inside and open to the message that will be there—from you yourself to you yourself. This may not be easy and you CAN stop at any time and look and see what is really going on.

Life is made up of a series of events that we ourselves have maestro'ed into existence for the soul (no typo) purpose of living our lives to the fullest.

You don't need to take my word for it. Check it out—look and see what messages you have orchestrated for yourself. The messages can come from anyone, anything, no one, and nothing…they all count. The point here is, to stop and receive these messages—to be there for your Self.

When the details that are happening are strong—emotions flying, loud discomfort…these will be the messages where you are really making the felt experience exaggerated so you will notice: "Hey, something is happening!" Rarely does it have to do with what it appears to be on the surface. Stop and feel yourself inside, open to receive the message(s) from you, from life herself.

Letting Go Specifically

This week's invitation is to look at, and practice, letting go, specifically, whatever it is you are holding in your own way of: more love; more abundance; more money; more peace; or the fully awakened state of Being.

For instance, if there is a living in the survival state (money worries) then it would be a letting go of whatever is in your own way of effortless abundance. A full commitment to letting go of whatever that is, without knowing, unconditionally—faulty beliefs, fear of wealth, judgment of money, or fear of success (to name just a few). All of these could block a natural flow of monetary wealth. It's not about "having" it; it is about it just being an easy part of your life, an easy flow. You get to play with it! In other words, you fully, with all of your heart, commit to letting go of whatever energy is blocking you and then let the Universe take care of it by inviting you on what wants to happen.

Inviting a letting go of whatever is in your way of being in the fully Realized State of Awareness is a wonderful commitment to make—letting go of ideas, emotions, and various energies that may have been keeping you anchored in a state of imagined separation.

Practice giving yourself space in letting go of whatever is in your own way to affluence, to joy, to love, to spiritual fulfillment, to an easy and contented way of living.

Practical Surrender

This week's invitation is to embrace your own "Power." It is rather odd to call it "yours" as really it belongs to Source like all else. And, you were given this life to tend to, to learn in, to learn mastery with everything, and to enjoy and relax into That.

This week's invitation is practical surrender to What Is. Allowing yourself to sit and feel (to surrender to) whatever is happening.

This can be easy when it is a pleasurable experience, however, often there can be resistance if the experiencing is unpleasant, or out of one's comfort zone. The invitation is to open up and allow yourself to simply experience whatever it is, no matter what.

If "irritation" is what you are feeling, stop, sit down and feel irritation happening. Stop trying to stop it or override it by doing something. Sit and feel the irritation, witness it as energy.

If you are feeling "anger" or "grief," sit and feel it, do nothing except stop movement, close your eyes, relax open, breathe and feel it—surrender to it and see what happens. If "trying" is happening, stop and feel the energy of "trying." Or "overwhelm" is a common one too—feeling "overwhelmed" what does overwhelm energy actually feel like? Feel these very human energies instead of attempting to change them or override them...stop, open and surrender by resting with the experience which is happening.

This invitation is to surrender to What Is and feel it fully. Perhaps in the first time, perhaps after a few times, the grief, anger, irritation, or whatever will melt away leaving you—the peace and love that you are.

CHAPTER SEVEN

Every Moment Invites You

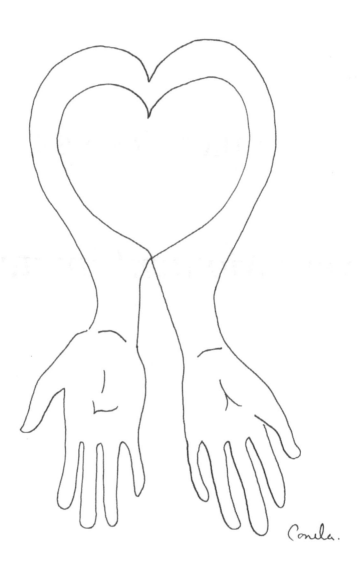

Conela.

From the place of Being, you your Self is constantly
inviting yourself into more of yourself.
What a sentence!

Everyone, whether they realize it or not, is in a state of Being.
As That, Consciousness is always attempting expansion of itself—
to express more of its Self.

Perhaps you may recognize this as you look back on the moments
that you have experienced, that you have grown and expanded
simply through living.

The magnitude of this growing and expanding can relate
to how many of the invitations
(which appear to be from Life)
you actually engage in.

The invitations in this chapter
invite you to recognize these
invitations from life in each moment,
to trust them even more as they are
coming from such a beloved space...
from you yourself.

Taking Action

This invitation is to play around with Taking Action. There is so much that is read, is spoken, is brought to each person's attention (if they are interested) of what the "Truth" is, and what supports That.

The temptation might be to simply agree with what is written...perhaps feel the truth in the words and then, therefore, agree with it. Sometimes that is the case and that is what is being invited by Consciousness.

Many, many times, though, the invitation really is to "take action" and try out what is being offered for yourself, to directly experience the effect of what is being invited. It doesn't matter if you misinterpret the invitation because your very way of interpreting it is vital to whatever action you may take. What is important is that it sounds true to you and that is enough to try it out.

So many people just nod their heads and say, "that sounds true" and so few people actually take action on what is being offered—actually try it out for themselves to see if what the words are inviting is actually true for them. The part that makes something true or not is the direct experience of it...your direct experience. If you don't try it out you cannot really know if it is true or not. And yes, this is the part that is often not so easy, is often very vulnerable, or is perhaps uncomfortable.

When you do take action and try it out for yourself, then the experience becomes a part of Reality…it becomes Realized, or Real, and this is embodiment. Piece by piece, bit by bit, step by step, and moment by moment—the Self is embodied, is Realized.

Taking action is being invited: play with engagement and disengagement of the mind; allow your attention to rest with what you are actually experiencing; share the Real experience of yourself; simply Be yourself and experience That directly—go beyond concepts in the head to directly experiencing one's Self.

Looking for Love in All the Right Places

This week's invitation is one of "Being With" Love. From this perspective of Canela, Love is all there is. Love Consciousness makes up the entire play of what is happening—the thoughts, the actions, the manifested molecules as things, the breath, the play of it all—from its Self to its Self.

And how is this an invitation? You are invited to look again, in any moment, to see if you can allow the Love that Is. That the Love is here, is a given…it's just that sometimes it seems disguised.

It may take some courage to let go of what seems to be happening and open to the possibility that it is Love expressing itself to you. When the moment feels uncomfortable and emotions might be running high, these are the most powerful moments to stop and open your body, your mind, your being, to the expression of Love in that very moment.

Is this easy? Perhaps not at first. Yet once you get the hang of it, it becomes an easier choice—to let go of any habitual "known" pathway like: hanging on to being right; defending your position; proving the other is wrong; the details are not good or should be some other way than they are…basically saying "No!" to whatever is happening. You are invited to stop, breath, open your body and tune in to the very moment of your experience. Let go of the details (you can always pick them up again later if you want) and feel yourself, open yourself, and even ask the question: Is this Love? Not to judge the moment, rather to actually allow a space to feel into it: is Love happening right now? Such curiosity will provoke an answer... a felt experience.

This is an opportunity to tune into the Love that exists, here for you, in each moment—to experience this directly.

Wahe Guru / The Guru Within

This invitation is very simple: "Wahe Guru." It is the invitation from and to yourself, within you and without, yet usually ignited "within" first, then the "without" is understood in its inclusion.

All of these Satsang Invitations are in support of Wahe Guru —the Guru within you. Attending Satsang with Canela, and all of the formats of support offered with her, are totally in support of you being connected to That. That is why she isn't really a teacher; instead she is a supporter of what you already are. Being in the presence of That which is Realized, magnifies That so it is easier and more obvious to experience.

The invitation to play with, whether you end up attending the Satsang gatherings in person or not, is to connect more and more with Wahe Guru. This amazing, wise, all-encompassing Guru is with you in each moment, is beckoning to you from within and without. It only requires your interest and/or curiosity, for you to turn toward your Self instead of being tranquilized by spending your attention on the details of life and the ideas around those details that are not what they seem to be. The temptation has been (perhaps) to be drawn into the drama of the details, to categorize them, then let the mind run on with it while you listen to whatever the mind comes up with.

Wahe Guru invites you to let go, in the moment, of following the temptations and instead to feel into what is happening—which connects you to the Guru within, which connects you with All That Is.

Experiences Come and Go

The invitation here is to notice that experiences come and go. Throughout your lifetime, you can see that you have had all sorts of experiences and none of them have ever repeated. There might be similarities with some of them, and never are they the same. There also might be a tendency to attempt to repeat certain experiences. You may be aware of these tendencies or not, up until now. What is a great support to yourself, is to recognize that you are attempting to have some experience repeat itself.

Common experiences that people can get attached to are experiences where they felt safe and loved. They go in search of replicating the outside details so that they might create the same experience, like when they felt safe and cared for as a small child, having someone at your beck and call to take care of you like your mother or father. So one then goes along and attempts to find a partner or mate who would take care of you and be at your beck and call like how it was when you were a child and all was taken care of. You might find, again and again, that the apparent "other" just won't give you that feeling.

Sometimes the experiences are ones that might be called "spiritual" where one feels touched by God or Goddess, in direct contact with their Higher Self.

It is so human to attach these experiences to the details that happen to be present at that moment, the time, the place, the circumstances. Often parts of those details do support such experiences, but they will never be exactly the same and to recreate them is impossible, since you yourself are changing in each and every moment and so is all of life.

The invitation is to let go of the experiences, allowing gratitude that you did experience them, then let them go. Allow space for new experiences to come to you.

People tend to attach to such experiences because they are special to them, they do mean something to them and have likely changed their lives. However, experiences come and go; holding onto them as if they were "something" can be in the way of you hearing life invite you to new spiritual experiences. Let go of the attachment to the experience, letting the experience be what it is—not dismissing it or minimizing it, just that it has already occurred. This will leave yourself available for whatever comes next.

Yes, letting go of any attempt (once you are aware of it) to repeat an experience, will leave space for Life to invite you in each moment even more deeply.

CHAPTER EIGHT

Being Groovy with You

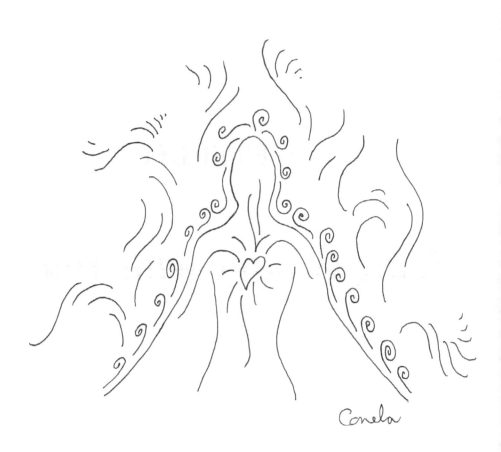

Feeling Groovy!
There are moments when groovy is happening,
a free spirit feeling, like the inside is dancing along with the out-
side —all is in harmony.

Over time, it has been found that this feeling groovy feeling is
always available no matter
what the moment looks like.

That in relaxing open to whatever is happening,
(being with That consciously)
even traumatic experiences can end up
being another invitation of loving yourself;
of being groovy with you.

Accepting your humanness, no matter what, has that result—
that it's pretty groovy to be human.

Great Fullness

G reat Fullness is such a wonderful and rich topic for this week's invitation. The invitation is to spend some time with yourself allowing moments that have happened in the apparent past, to rise into your "Now."

Specifically call on moments of direct experiencing of thankfulness, or gratefulness—grateful for a beautiful day; great and full to be alive; grateful that you are you; grateful that you are connected to the family that you are—parents, siblings, children; grateful for winning anything; moments that you felt on top of the world. Let them rise in you, be with you now. Spend some time with gratefulness like this. Feel how your energy may shift, what happens inside?

Allow these energies to permeate your whole being—every cell, your whole personal energy field, then let them expand out and beyond into all. Perhaps you might share the energy with people that you know who could use some support in their lives. Let these people rise to heart and share this experience with you. Notice what happens when you allow this; how do you feel now? Perhaps you might feel even more full and alive? Doesn't the experience coincide with the words: great fullness, thank fullness? This is what it is to be thankful; it's a happening.

You'll Do It Your Way!

This invitation to yourself is a reminder that "Your Way" is the "right way" for you. In the title of this invitation above, imagine that Frank Sinatra is singing this to you! You are the only One who is perceiving life as yourself. No one else can possibly know all of the moments that have been experienced by you; what it is like to look like you; to sound like you; to hear like you; to taste like you; to see like you. This is the incredible gift of your life—so uniquely yours and yours alone. It also comes with a responsibility, because no one else will have your "answers." You can resonate with others, feel drawn to experience modes of healing, hear another's words interpreted by you, and perhaps even initiating action by you.

This is what Jesus meant when he said "Do as I say, not as I do." Copying what he did, or what Buddha did, may have its own reward but it will not be your awakening. It may contribute to That, but what they "did" was follow their own way to Self. They followed their own steps to that. You have your own way, your own feet, your own way of thinking, perceiving. Follow what feels right to you from inside of yourself in any moment. The answer of "your way" lies in each moment—for you to choose, left or right? Which feels to be the right way to you? This is living righteously.

It is an invitation for you to hear yourself; to feel your "right way"; to practice tuning into the very moment; and perhaps to share what that might feel like with others. It is not to cancel out the human experience—it is to celebrate it, embrace it, relax into it, Be That...no matter what, unconditionally, however you Are. You are so welcome!

Unusual Gratitude

This week's invitation is one of Gratitude towards that which already is. It is "unusual" in spending some moments being grateful toward parts of yourself which have been in play and perhaps not acknowledged or appreciated very often…until now!

Parts like elbows, shin bones, the cartilage that is part of the spine, balance, the magical workings of the brain, the felt sense of everything—like bare feet on a soft rug. Have you spent time experiencing the wonder of being able to see, smell, hear, taste?

Now is a great time for this. The parts of the play of what is that are mentioned above are just pointed to to nudge you in your own direction…and they might be what you would like to spend time with…it is up to you.

Sit quietly, breathe deeply and relax your body. Put your hands on your elbows, or perhaps one at a time and just recognize what a gift they are to you in your life…how much you can do because, lo and behold, there are elbows there as part of your arms. Go through whatever parts of yourself that you would like to give some gratitude attention to…parts of yourself that may have never been acknowledged before now.

So much is given and received in each and every moment—gratitude can rise simply by acknowledging what is. It's a natural side effect. What a win-win situation!

Setting Yourself Up
for Magnificence

I invite you, to start your day, from right now (and any day that it may occur to you) to invite yourself to experience magnificence.

Go to a mirror...I mean the real mirror, that reflective glass on the wall. Look into those eyes that see you, that see the person standing there, the magnificence of simply seeing. Seeing too, the flesh; that each molecule has its own intelligence to know itself as part of the skin—totally magnificent! Trillions of them all knowing, agreeing, to continue Being together as your skin. Let in the magnificence of that! Nothing at all except for that magnetic intelligence holds "you" together in one "peace."

The magnificence of the blood that runs through your veins, transporting nutrients throughout the body—intricately, perfectly, without you "doing" a single thing. Same as the breath, going in, going out, a simple movement that sends oxygen throughout the system—feeding aliveness into you, into your brain tissue, that then receives all the information, inside and out, that gives you the experience of Being Alive. That is, truly magnificent!

See what happens in your day, your moments, when you invite magnificence to be experienced.

CHAPTER NINE

It's OK to Be Human

Over and over again, it is seen that people mistake
the spiritual search as one that transcends
the parts of existence that look human.

What actually occurs in transcendence is the perception
of all that is happening, including the part of existence that
looks human, changes. The human aspect is no longer seen as a
hindrance. It is recognized for what it is and therefore no longer
creates suffering as a result. The human's life carries on just as it
was prior, although of course the happenings are so much lighter
as one knows that those details are not the big deal they might
once have seemed to be—attachment is gone.

This mistake is an easy one to make as before transcendence,
it appears that it is the human looking parts of life that are
causing the suffering. When the truth is, it is how those human
plays are being perceived that ignites the suffering.

The perception is what changes, not the details of the human being
—whether there is lots of money or friends or recognition. These
things just no longer hold the importance that perhaps they once
did so they no longer have the same effect. We can use the pull
towards these items—lots of money, friends or recognition,
to support us to more and more awareness. Going with them,
instead of attempting to grab hold of them or push them
away because they don't appear to be spiritual.

Motivation for Change

This invitation is to look at, and be with, what is motivating you when you are inviting something to change. So many motivations are ones that do not serve your Self or anyone. As an example, motivations to attempt to stop the aging process or anything done with the motivation to attempt to change your body into whatever you imagine it "should" look like, is attempting to stop What Is. Or even motivation to ignite the "drug" of adrenaline, to get your fix, when swimming or running for example, is not a healthy motivation.

On the other hand, honouring the body's natural pull towards something is really being with the body in the moment, so the motivation in this case, is in support of all that is.

Just look at whether you are motivated by some idea of the mind to look different—or that you "have to" because of an addiction—or is it an actual pull of the body to rejoice in its self through swimming, or hiking, healthy food, or whatever it is that entices in the moment? Here, once again, there is a dependency on your own honesty with yourself. If you find "convincing" happening, you are likely not being totally honest.

As you look at this, and perhaps register with yourself some of your own motivations that may not be the healthiest, it is not about calling yourself "wrong." It is simply about looking at this to see what has been happening, and then letting go of attempting to change anything about yourself, or another, that is stemming from motivation that is against yourself as a natural human being.

Once you have stopped pushing, pulling, or contorting yourself to look like something else, there can be a relaxing into this way that the molecules rest together as this body, really relaxing open to how this body is right now—letting go of judging it as not being how you want it to be; softening with yourself and registering that this is simply how it is…the body has an easier time to function and becomes much more healthy and vibrant.

Yes, the funny thing is, when you really trust how the body shows up to be, it relaxes into being more youthful because there is no longer stress or strain for it to be different than it is. You may even notice people where wrinkles are present, and see how beautiful they are regardless of the signs of the body aging, especially if they are people who have accepted the natural course of things and are no longer fighting What Is.

The Guest That You Are

This week's invitation is to consider that you are a guest here in this experience of Being human. A guest in this body, with this mind, this energy that is yours to play in, this set of details—be you man or woman, mother, father, brother, sister. A guest with this mother, this father, brother, uncle, aunty, friend...these have all been given to you. This space that you call your home, your abode, this space that you know as your Home inside...this heart, this soul...can you see any part of what is happening that has not been given to you to experience? This Space of "you," experiencing something, experiencing whatever it is that is happening, inclusive of all details.

This invitation is to treat this body, this mind, this energy with respect...just as a guest would. Is any of it really "yours"?

Do you respect the son, daughter, cat, foot, sock, which has happened to land in this life with you, given to you to experience, to Be With? Being with this range of emotions, this flavor of being, this character...simply all of it.

What is your way of respecting, appreciating, all of this?

Include Yourself

This invitation is one that seems so obvious, yet not very many people actually follow through on: include yourself. When decisions are made, they are often made around others and do not include the very best thing that could happen for you yourself. Loving our children, they come first; loving our partners, they come first; believing that we have to in order to survive, the job comes first. Somewhere down the line, maybe we can clear a space to spend time and attention on ourselves? You may find that this doesn't tend to happen very often.

This invitation is to include yourself in all of your decisions. When looking at going out to pick up a son or daughter, is it really the best thing for you? Do you do so because you imagine you "have to" or because you actually feel like doing so? Of course they do need to come home, perhaps they can catch a bus or there is someone who is already picking up their children who could include yours. Or maybe it is time for them to take a taxi home. To trust that it is affordable compared with trespassing against yourself.

Sometimes the decision to include yourself needs to happen at the onset of a commitment. As an example, like when deciding how many extracurricular activities your child signs up for. On one hand, you want them to experience a lot, and on the other, who wants to be a taxi driver without pay? Because so many parents just do it, the younger people expect it, often feeling even entitled to your time and energy. If you don't bother to include yourself, it is pretty much guaranteed that they won't, and it's not their fault; it's what you model. You have taught them to treat you like that, as if that is how it is supposed to be—that you transgress against yourself for their sake. Is that really loving? To who? To teach your children when they become parents to transgress against themselves? Look at what is being modeled and you will see where this whole cycle begins.

Often the over load of commitments that children have, teach them to continue to do so into adulthood. It creates a comfort zone that is unhealthy. Is it no wonder then when eventually they are so exhausted? Perhaps it might even look a lot like the exhaustion parents feel when they continually override being loving toward themselves.

Do you have the courage to end the cycle, to include yourself and be loving to yourself in each and every decision? It may mean that your kids, partner, or employer will be surprised at first, if they have been used to you throwing away your time and energy, and, it is not the end of the world.

When you do include yourself (by including whether each decision is truly loving toward yourself and taking action accordingly) you will find that it always works out much better for everyone. This is not something to just think about, it is something to actually try out so you can see for yourself how it works. Show yourself by your own example that it does, indeed, work out better for everyone included.

Start with taking some moments when you are about to do something and you already feel tired just with the thought of it. Take a few moments to sit with yourself and look at how loving an action is it that you are about to take, how loving is it for you yourself?

A great way to figure out if it is loving for you or not, is to imagine that the same decision is one that someone you love needs to take. Often, people can see what the most loving choice is for someone else—for their son or daughter, good friend, sister, or brother. Just imagine that it is them that is making the decision about the action. In your love of them, would you have them take that action or not?

When you are loving to you, you are loving to the whole Universe, as you are a representation, or expression, of That. When you trespass against yourself out of some idea of "how you are supposed to be," well, then, this is what you offer the Universe and model for your children to live in the same way. We are all part of One, so you can trust that when you do the most loving thing inclusive of yourself, it actually includes the whole Universe.

CHAPTER TEN

Acceptance

You have been accepted.
The fact that you exist at all shows
this acceptance because you are
currently taking up the space of "you."

As all is totally connected; you exist as part of all that is.
To not accept your self is really
quite odd as it would mean that there is a
non-acceptance of all that is.

It is only ideas or beliefs that have been
energized over time that lay between you and
total acceptance of yourself.

Unravel this over time...take your time,
take space for yourself, allow yourself to relax open
to the truth of this fact of your existence—
that there is, in fact, an experience happening
and you as awareness are with it—
you have been accepted
in every single moment
of this lifetime.

Being in Grace

This invitation is one of Grace. Grace is non-judgmental, unconditional, sweetly embracing, and is such a beautiful direction of surrender—to surrender to Grace.

Consider that Grace is available in each moment: that you eat food in grace, talk in grace, read books in grace, think in grace, sleep in grace, walk in grace, breath in grace. Grace is always present no matter what it is that is happening. Being aware of this can be supportive...after all, if one were to remember that even arguments happen in grace, especially in the midst of them, wouldn't that take the edge off of them?

Remembering that breathing is happening in grace...well, now that you are reminded, how do you feel to be breathing in grace?

That there is this whole system called the human body is totally grace. That there is a brain at all is grace. Even that Awareness is aware of itself is grace. It's funny too, as to be grateful to grace for "all that is"—the gratefulness is grace itself.

Acceptance of You

This week's invitation is to look at, and allow yourself to taste Acceptance of You. A way that this can happen, without you "doing" anything, is to relax open and notice that something is Aware of you.

Something is Aware of the thoughts that might be happening, of the sensations in the body that might be happening, of the felt sense of gravity, of any emotions that might be occurring.

That "something" has accepted you long before you started thinking about whether or not you are accepted here. You have been accepted all along by the very fact of your existence. You have been heard all along, you have been seen all along, something has been interested in you and all that you experience in each and every moment. Awareness has been with you.

Some call this God; Goddess; Existence; Consciousness; Higher Self; Tao; Awareness. Whatever you call this, it has been with you, aware of you, listening to you, seeing you—all of your thoughts, actions, experiences—nothing at all has been missed by Awareness.

Check it out...see if you can feel Awareness listening to you, seeing you. This is beyond the mind and yet it is also aware of when thoughts are happening; it is aware of the mind too. If you give that some space to be felt, you just might hear, feel, and/or sense an answer.

Let It Be

This week's invitation is to—as the Beatles invite: Let it Be. Let "what" Be? Let the body be, let the mind be, let yourself be, let the other be...relax open to what is, exactly as it is.

All of this attempting to change everything by demand; this non-acceptance of "How It Is," is a waste of energy, because all it is, is a bunch of molecules dancing together as a body, or thoughts, or air, or sound, or whatever...a part of this great illusion that is dancing itself, revealing itself to this apparent "you" part of itself.

Notice an arm as it is; a thought as it is; let it just be itself. Stop attempting to stop those thoughts or contort the body into some societal "norm" of how a woman or a man is "supposed to look." Tending to these things, yes...perhaps there is a feeling of thirstiness; yes, well, have a drink of water...a feeling to speak, then let it be, let speaking happen. The feeling will be light, be a preference, not a demand.

Letting it be (whatever "it" is) is surrender, is acceptance. For example, if "thirstiness" is what is happening, then be with that appropriately and have a drink of water. "What is" includes you as a human being and all of the possibilities that go along with that.

A way to know if there is a surrendering to what is (or is

it an attempt to move away from "what is" by attempting to change it?) is by feeling your energy and being honest in the moment with yourself. Are you attempting to push, pull or control anything or anyone? If you notice any pushing, pulling or controlling, stop the action of it. You can relax the energy that is pushing or pulling…stop the push or the pull by relaxing it, and let the energy just be, let it be.

Controlling

This week's invitation is to look at being "controlling." What is that and how do you know if you are being controlling, or freely moving with focus (which may look like "controlling" on the outside)?

Control is often the opposite of freedom or going with the flow. When your computer shuts down three times in a row, it's time to let go, relax, and not attempt to "make it" work...it doesn't want to happen right then. Look for what does want to happen with curiosity.

The answer to "how do you know if you are being controlling?" is simple, yet not always easy to assess—it is to be honest with yourself.

If there is any defense—is the mind coming up with all sorts of reasons as to why your actions are not controlling?—the likelihood is very high that you are indeed attempting to control something. Freely moving with focus doesn't have any push to it, it's just happening, defense just doesn't even come up.

Controlling anything usually accompanies some sort of feeling of push or pull—someone is "trying" to do something, or to change "what is" through force. If something "has to" happen in a certain way, or someone "should be" acting differently than they are, then there is attempt to control happening. This is simply getting in your own way. Even though it looks "right" or is perfectly logical, you will be swimming upstream, rather than flowing along with what is.

Judging another as controlling is often an indicator that you yourself have some sort of aspect of control happening, especially if you feel that you need to tell the other that they are being controlling. If they are, let them find it out for themselves. Just notice it in your own awareness, no need to speak of it. If that urge to "have to tell them" is with you, then stop and see what part of you is controlling something right in that moment. Relax your body open and ask the question inwardly to see what response you get.

As with absolutely everything, it is not "wrong" to attempt to control anything; it's just not the best for you and uses up a lot more of your energy. Finding yourself "attempting to control" is, however, a great invitation to be able to follow it inside, feel it, let go of the pushing or pulling energy and learn more about yourself and your own way of being…always expanding on That.

CHAPTER ELEVEN

Belonging Here

*In the play of being human, most of us were taught through the
modeling of people around us that everything is separate. That
that which is seen is made up of separate "things"—
including ourselves.*

*This is taught innocently, and mostly subconsciously.
That even though we might belong to a family, or a business,
or some sort of group or another, our "belonging" appears
to be attached to the continuance of the group, person,
or circumstance outside of ourselves.*

*In the experiencing of ourselves as part of all that is,
the question of belonging or not no longer exists.
Yes, there is an aloneness in the experience because
it is uniquely your own (no one else is experiencing life
exactly like you are) and in the same moment, all
that is being experienced is felt and
seen to be connected...if one only looks.*

*It is a straight ahead fact, not just an idea that sounds pretty.
It is the real feeling of security—to feel that connectedness
simultaneously with our uniqueness...the full, real, and
everlasting experience of belonging that
never, ever changes.*

Team of One

This week, the invitation is to allow yourself to sense and feel yourself as part of the Team of One. Open to allowing the Universe itself to support you.

As you are reading this, just after reading this very sentence, stop and see if you can open your senses to feel the Universe being with you. It may take some moments to relax open so you can "hear" this support through felt sense. Open up your body, mind, and energy field...letting go of any idea of an edge where you end and the rest of the Universe begins, let that edge go and feel, directly, how completely connected you are.

You are not alone, you are part of everything that is, everything is connected—you have heard all of this before, and now I invite you to actually feel this, to open up and allow yourself to feel supported by your team, the team of One that everyone belongs to.

You are not separate from all that is, you are part of it, and all happenings are completely connected. You are not handling things on your own, you never were, and you never will be. Shrug off those ideas, relax open, and feel the support that is with you in each moment.

As you allow yourself to feel this—to relax open enough to feel this—the Universe has more space to take care of all that needs to be taken care of. When you are required to take action, the Universe will send you a repeating message, which can get more and more uncomfortable until you listen and follow through for yourself.

The Universe, in its wonderful way of Being with us, finds exactly what wants to happen next from inside of ourselves and offers it to us, invites us, sends us its message again and again until we listen.

You are invited to explore this and give yourself the space to feel the support that has been there/here for you all along and always will be.

Here is Where You Have Been Going To

This invitation is one of acceptance of where you are. Relax open and let go of any apparent goal to reach, recognize and experience where you are as where you have been going to up until Now.

Living in demand always has some sort of goal about an apparent future, or an attempt to move away from an apparent past. Instead, relax open to Now.

Whatever needs to be healed from the apparent past, as well as whatever is coming to you from the apparent future, will arise within and without, here now. There is no place to get to, there are no issues that have to be looked for to be healed, just relax open to yourself now, as completely as you are able, and whatever needs to happen, will. You do not need to look for it, simply give it the space (by relaxing open) to arise, then tend to it; be with it as is appropriate.

Life becomes a tending to What Is, rather than a struggle to get somewhere.

Support the strengthening of your ability to relax open to who and where you are Now by practicing, or allowing That.

What is Here?

This invitation is to look at what is here, what remains the same throughout this lifetime. What does remain, is this human who is experiencing life.

You yourself change a lot as you travel through the moments of life, and then there is a part of you that remains the same. Look back on your experiencing of when you were a child and notice that the same one who noticed all that is happening is the very same one who is reading these words now, that there is a part of you that has been aware of all that is happening and you have been aware of this part of you and know that it exists, and that this part has always remained the same.

We hear people speak of this often: "Even though I have turned fifty, or sixty, or seventy-three, I am still the same person, I still feel to be the same as I have always been."

What that part of you is, is Awareness: Awareness being aware of all that has been occurring in your unique flavour of humanness at play in each moment.

That you yourself remain as a human during this lifetime is true too. I haven't heard yet of someone morphing into something other than what we call human. "You" are still here, reading this invitation.

You are Here. It is a fact that you belong, because here you are. You don't need to be invited, you just are. You cannot be excluded from the human race. You may feel excluded from time to time, and there will also be moments where you are not even thinking about whether or not you belong here. You may just be living your life participating in it however you are. That participation is a given, is a gift, no matter if you appear to be "doing" something or not, or thinking or not.

Just sitting still breathing—something is happening and something is aware that something is happening. You are all of the parts of That.

CHAPTER TWELVE

"With"ness

Conela.

Being With.

This is what is happening in each and every moment.
You are with this body, this mind, this personality,
this energy field, this scenario.

With it, however it is, no matter what.
This is what I call "With"ness—recognizing that
since you are already with all that is,
you may as well relax into it,
and enjoy it all even more.

Who is it that is With all that is?
Take a look and find out...who is it that is
aware of all that you are with
in this very moment
of reading this?

Recognizing "Truth"

This week's invitation to see and experience what is known as "The Truth." There are many ideas about what 'The Truth' is, how it is supposed to look. And the truth about the truth is, that it is absolutely all that is…including the thoughts, including apparent mistakes, including pain, including the mind, including yes and including no, including emotions and all of the states of Being—That which is occurring in each moment.

Instead of thinking about what the Truth is, take a look and experience it…right now. These words are before you, you are reading them, they are the Truth—that they are here "with you" on the page of this book; words have shown up to Be With you. It is not necessarily what they are saying; it is that they exist right now, here. The eyes that see them are also part of it; the whole action of "reading happening" is part of it; the body in the chair that you are experiencing simultaneously is it—both the body and the chair and the pressure felt where they meet; the breathing is it; the awareness that you are in fact reading is it…this right here, right now, is The Truth.

As you may be able to tell, it is an experience, not an idea. Whatever the experience is, from your own perspective, is the Truth of what is—there is something that is aware of the fact that you are experiencing something…it is before the mind, and includes it. To say it is "before" is not totally true as it is together in the same instant, yet this awareness includes it.

Any ideas of the Truth being one thing and another thing not being the Truth, are just ideas and not true. I invite you to drop the ideas and Be With what you are Aware of, what is actually happening, what is occurring, what arises Now.

Satsang at Home

This week, there is an offering of a couple of invitations. These invitations are in further response to a question that arose during Satsang. The question was something like: "How can I experience this feeling of Being in Satsang when I am at home in the midst of my day to day activities?"

For this, I invite you to slow down while in the midst of your actions. The tricky part about actions is that a person is often tempted to focus on finishing the action, instead of experiencing themself within the happening. Slow down and stay in touch with your heart while the action is happening. This can take some practice, as it may be a habit to be focused on the end result —completing the task, rather than experiencing the moments as they are happening.

Another invitation is to go along with whatever mundane thing is happening…watching TV perhaps. Instead of having your attention focused on the TV, let yourself relax open, feel yourself in your chair (the felt sense of the body), then let the information that is emanating from the screen, come to you. Let it come into your eyes, into your ears, instead of a sort of reaching out with your attention towards the TV. This can also be played with while on the computer, reading a book, or any happening —let that which appears to be "outside" of you, come "in" to you, effortlessly.

The other part of this is to let go of whatever was experienced in Satsang with Canela or others in its real details—as what has passed, has passed, and your experiencing of Satsang wherever you are will always be new, and then new again. Also, with a group of people who are united in intention—to experience the Truth of themselves, the experiencing of one's Self is magnified and can, therefore, be easier to "find" or experience directly.

With your own Self, it will likely be more subtle at first—as a part of you is already familiar with this (and always has been), it may feel not as obvious, or may feel much more ordinary. There may be a tendency to not count presence when experiencing the more ordinary details of life. Really, it is available no matter where you are, no matter what is happening, no matter who you are with.

The Gift

Imagine that someone gave you a gift, one that enabled you to experience life on earth in all of its variations. You were provided with a vehicle that would run itself as long as you kept care of it by feeding and watering it, keeping it clean and healthy, and listening to it by learning its language on all levels so it could tell you what it needs.

The gift includes an amazing computer system, connected to an energy system, which together could allow a multitude of information in many, many forms to come into the system, be digested and integrated.

The whole vehicle is powered by, and made up of something called Consciousness and costs each person absolutely nothing. The game being offered is to journey along, with something called time and to learn how to Be With each scenario as it presents itself.

Each scenario is also powered by, and made up, of this Consciousness stuff. If there is not an allowing to Be With each scenario in totality, the scenario will play itself again, and again, with a few details changed, until the person is able to Be With it totally, and therefore receive the learning; then the next scenario would begin.

Each new understanding would not be just for the person, but would also benefit the whole of Consciousness as it would

153

therefore be that much more aware of itself, and of course, there is no separation.

Part of the game is that each person is fed a misleading idea, the idea being that if they focused on attempting to change the scenario, instead of allowing themselves to Be With it, they could fix it.

This invitation is one that invites you to let go of that idea and "Be With" what is happening for you in your life as it is. Just as it is.

Find Out Who

This week's invitation is to explore who it is that is experiencing life right now. Find Out Who…Who is it that is directing this life experience? Who is it that is listening to this direction? Come and find out by experiencing this directly.

To expand on this and explore how to look for Who it is that you are, right now, follow these steps:

As you are reading these words, notice that reading is happening, something knows this—that reading is happening. Can you see that? That reading is happening?

Stop now and look to see who it is that is reading. You can see the page out here in front of you; you can feel where your eyes are that are looking. Relax open to all of that and now, look to see where is that part of you that is aware of all of this that is happening?

There is a "you," in your chair—you can feel your feet in socks, or slippers, or maybe barefoot against the floor—wherever your feet are…there they are, you can feel them, you are aware of them. And isn't that the same for the rest of your body? You can feel that there is a body right here, right now, as you read this.

Now, what is that that is aware of those feet? What is that that is aware of how they feel on the inside, the outside, energetically, physically? Look to see what part of you is aware of all of that.

This part that you are looking for is only available right in the moment of looking. It is here in each moment, never leaves, is always aware of everything, and can only be "found" through experiencing it in the very moment.

CHAPTER THIRTEEN

Saying "Yes" to You

There is a difference between "Yes" and
"No" that can be felt quite directly.

Close your eyes, feel your body sitting there, and say
"Yes" inside of yourself...perhaps just imagining the word "Yes"
travelling throughout your body.

Now do the same thing with the word "No."
One feels quite different than the other.

This is the same thing with the rest of life.

The tricky part can be to include yourself in your "yes."
For instance, you may feel a genuine "no" towards eating eggs that
someone offers you—you would be saying "yes" to yourself by
declining the offer of eggs.

So you see that it is not a "rule" that can be made...
to say "yes" to everything that comes your way.
Say "yes" to yourself, inclusive of the details in the moment,
and see what happens in your life.

"Self" Motivation

When issues arise in the midst of living your life, how you dance with them is so important in this embracing Awareness, this embracing one's Self. How is it that one person will face every fear that comes along, because they know that it will only surface in another place, in another way if it is not faced now? Such a person may know to not waste their time and energy in attempting to change the outside details in an attempt to avoid feeling whatever it is that needs to be felt. What motivates One to embrace themselves with deep, cleansing honesty?

If I had the recipe, I am sure I would paste on every website, send it out on the radio and TV, tell every person I meet about it and give them a copy of the recipe…what a difference it would make in this Universe!

Instead, I am left with acknowledging those who do take those courageous steps towards themselves; those who understand that Now is the time to face whatever it is—in some new way, a way that the moment itself will suggest; to give that moment space and listen to what is actually occurring; to feel it—to follow the energy inside in order to set it free by feeling it.

I acknowledge all of you, you know who you are! I acknowledge your courage, your vulnerability, your willingness to be humbled and feel remorse if that is what comes. You know who you are; I acknowledge you in That.

And thank you, for embracing yourself instead of turning away from yourself. Thank you for making the world a more Loving place.

Allow More of Who You Are

This invitation is one that invites you to be more of who you are; to follow through on the little nudges that come from within, that perhaps, in the past, you may not have followed because you imagine that someone might judge you for it.

No one else is hearing them because they are for you alone. You yourself know when they have happened, when you have listened, and when you have not.

Sometimes these inner nudges are direct links to your own expansion. Choosing them, over fear, will result in expansion of you, learning, and most likely, a more alive and loving human (yourself) by saying "yes" to these nudges.

Support yourself to strengthen the courage to say "Yes" to yourself and act upon it. Everything is Consciousness. Deepen the awareness of this; release anything that might be in the way of experiencing That.

Action Towards Maximum Potential

This invitation is for the ignition of action toward supporting your own Maximum Potential. Commit to taking action that supports your Maximum Potential. Without knowing what that might be, be as sincere as you can be and commit to it—whatever that is, so there can be more of the play of You, alive and well, flourishing on this earth.

In those moments when you hold yourself back, support your maximum potential instead by letting yourself do whatever it is that you were holding yourself back from. Instead of making yourself small, let yourself be large; not traipsing over others, just taking the space that appears before you that is being offered. It is a natural process, these taking of steps, feeling the space, recognizing the moment when you are being invited to step, and STEP.

As far as I can tell so far, it appears that that is what we are here for—to simply and as fully as possible—be the expression of Life that we are.

Maximum potential is a happening sort of thing as when it is touched or lived, it will expand again...so it is an ongoing expansion of you yourself living more and more of the potential of you.

Allowing Instead of Wanting

This invitation is to shift into allowing instead of wanting. Allow that which you have been holding away from yourself to finally arrive; allow a greater experience of feeling love; allow yourself to be loved even more deeply; allow yourself to trust yourself and your world even more; allow yourself to focus your attention on interests that serve you and the greater good; allow a shift in focus away from interests that do not serve you or the greater good; allow a melting away, a surrendering of ideas and beliefs that have only been held in your way of Being; allow yourSelf to Be that which you are—whatever that might be in any moment.

When "wanting" is happening, it creates energy held right in front of you—in other words, "wanting" is a happening that takes up its own space. An extension of your own energy will loom out before you toward that which you want. That energy that is looming out is the very energy that stops the item from being able to be with you.

Imagine something that you want to be right in front of you. Your energy of "want" will be right in between you and the thing that you would like when you are wanting it. Notice this and then shift to allowing. With the image of whatever it is you are wanting in front of you, let go of the wanting energy and instead open up your body to that image. Let the image merge with you, be with you, as you relax open to it…imagine that. In this way you are actually drawing whatever it is you want toward you instead of keeping it on the other side of the wanting energy, leaving a vacuum of space for that which you want to fall in with you.

CHAPTER FOURTEEN

Transform What You Don't Want into What You Do

Canela.

All is energy.
It's true...everything that is being sensed
in each moment is made up of energy.

This chapter invites you to Mastery of energy.
It may not mean mastery in
every single moment where it could be,
it does mean that you yourself gets to say
what happens with energy that is
related to you yourself.
To a certain degree that is. As sometimes,
events need to happen in such a way
to support the most for the most.
Life herself handles such events.

Where we can have a say though,
it can be fun, exciting,
and rather humbling to play with the energy
that is available to support the creation of
an even more enjoyable and relaxed
way of Being.

Pain is Energy

This week's invitation is to look at, and be with opening to pain (or any happening that is uncomfortable) as energy. If you are, or if you ever do experience pain, the invitation here is to remember that what you identify as "pain" is actually "energy" and can be opened to as that.

Often the discomfort with "pain" is the attempt to get rid of it, or move away from it. Any push on it will magnify and accentuate it—which is when people sometimes take painkillers in an attempt to not feel it. This works on a surface level to numb the experience yet it also loses the opportunity to explore what the energy is actually inviting in the moment. If you are making Consciousness or Awakening a priority in your life, then feeling "What Is" is the direction to go instead of masking it or avoiding it. Not to make taking pain killers "wrong," just supporting awareness of a different possibility or opportunity.

Instead of painkillers, the invitation is to open to the pain directly as energy and feel it. Relax the rest of your body open around the area of pain energy to give it some space to just be, breathe deeply, then "listen" to it by feeling it. You are experiencing it anyway, why not open to it and see what happens?

To repeat that: stop trying to stop the pain and instead

listen to it…give this a bit of time to allow yourself to relax into it. This is not a common way (yet) to respond to pain so it might take a bit more time to allow yourself to relax open to it.

Shifting the identification from the label of "pain" to "energy" can also lighten the intensity right away. The collective consciousness tends to attempt to get rid of "pain" whereas "energy" is more nondescript and is therefore easier to open to.

Following through by feeling this energy, being curious, and seeing what happens, is a way of being totally present.

This can work with any energy that you don't like (such as pain, irritation, frustration, overwhelm, disappointment, etc.). Remember that this too is simply energy that is present… be present to it by listening to it, stopping the push away and relaxing open to it instead. Any experience that you want to stop, as soon as you can diagnose that you don't like it (or diagnose that there is an attempt to stop it) is the time, in that moment, to stop, breathe deeply, and open to feeling it directly, right in the moment that it is found.

Halloween Happenings

This week's invitation is in celebration of Halloween! What a wonderful play of the illusion to be open to, and allow—with fun—giving the terrors of the darkness space to play. Here's the invitation: allow a space of time to journey into your own darkness, perhaps even terrors. It may feel appropriate for you to explore this with a good friend present.

To begin this exploration, it would be supportive to give yourself a bit of time to breathe and relax into yourself. Register that there is weight to the body and feel how gravity holds you in the chair (or wherever you are). With the felt sense of the body present, remind yourself that you are safe, within the room, and that you are a person who would like to meet with these "characters" on purpose, instead of waiting until they jump out at you from the dark.

Recognize this as an opportunity and simply allow them to unfold—to expose themselves to you as more of yourself. It is only when you hold them away, or attempt to avoid them, that they may loom into even bigger monsters that seem to threaten your very existence.

Relax open to the terrors, one by one bringing them up in thought, then allowing an unfolding...not engaging in them, just witnessing what happens—allowing yourself "as Awareness" to Be With these parts of who you are. After all, they are with you anyway; why not get more comfy with them?

Every little bit of life is part of Consciousness—Be With all of it, exactly how it is.

Alchemizing Energy

This invitation is to look at, and practice, alchemizing energy. In order to come to a point in your life that you can look forward to any kind of energy happening—be it anger, resentment, depression, fear, whatever it is that you would like to alchemize—learn how to put that energy into a statement supporting something that you would like more of in your life.

For instance, the next time that you find yourself angry, catch yourself in it, and then put that energy of anger into your statement.

Your statement can be anything that you would like, even if it is not happening yet, just something that you imagine that you would feel happy about if it were true. An example: "I love that I choose to focus on fitness and well-being! Over and over again I find myself making healthier and happier choices—I love that!"

Just try it out and see what happens—the anger will be changed, alchemized, into something else. You may even say it through gritted teeth at first, that's ok, just allow the anger energy to be felt, while at the same time putting it into the statement.

It is about being responsible for your own life, tending to That—allowing even more Mastery and having fun with energies that you didn't like before, becoming friends with these energies, with all of yourself.

Allowing Affluence

This week's invitation is Allowing Affluence—affluence of whatever you would like more of in your life. With many people, their relating with money is a grand learning opportunity. Instead of wondering why money is not with you or whether you deserve it or not, the invitation here is to look directly at how you relate to money itself.

Do you give money more power than other forms of Consciousness? After all, all forms are equal; it's only the power we give to the form that creates its effect with us. So now, bring your power home.

Power is energy; you gave it away, now you get to call it home.

A meditation: Put some money on a table in front of yourself, look at it, and allow whatever rises—thoughts, feelings, and sensations, notice that. Then, while still connecting directly to the money sitting there, open up your body and call "your energy" "home" from the money. "Your energy" is simply whatever attention you have been giving money; call it home to you, into the center of your Being.

Repeat this exercise whenever worries about money arise. At a minimum, you will be spending some time with money in a new way, instead of worrying about it, and at a maximum, your relationship with money will change and it will be much more freely flowing in your life.

Feel free to use this exercise with any part of life where perhaps your relationship is not in harmony yet.

Inviting Change

This week's invitation is to directly invite change in the details of your life. Do you have some sort of issue or challenge happening in your life that you would love to see change in?

Create a space of time for yourself, perhaps a half hour or so. Look at what you would like to change in your life. Take what is actually occurring and write down the opposite of that, whatever it is that you would like.

For example, if you have been experiencing tension at month's end over feeling uncertain if there will be enough financial resources to cover your costs, take that experience to muse on, and decide what the opposite of that experience would be.

It is important that you find your own words and way with this, and so I offer the following only as an example of what the opposite might be. Something like this:

> *"At the end of the month I feel full and satisfied, feeling so grateful that all of the bills are paid with grace and ease. How wonderful to be so supported by the details of life that everything is taken care of!"*

Now, feel that as if it were true…spend some moments imagining how you might feel with everything taken care of and with more than enough money to meet all of the costs of living.

You might find that all sorts of reasons to not allow yourself a space to be with this in this way, it would be natural that they might rise. Pay them no heed and do it anyway…what could it possibly hurt to spend time imagining and feeling the well-being that comes when any idea of lack is let go of. This feeling, allowing yourself to feel it, will magnetize more of that to you…more experiences of well-being, of ease and flow with life.

CHAPTER FIFTEEN

The Self

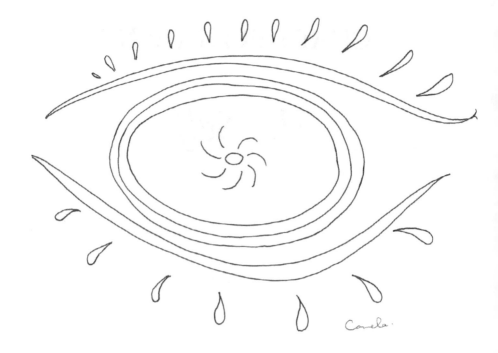

The "Self"... this word points to something that is not something
that you can see, touch, hear, taste or smell, as if it were a
"something" yet it includes all of those as
"happenings" in the moment.

That which is seen, and the seeing occurring, is the Self;
that which can be touched, and the touching happening, is the
Self;
that which can be heard, as well as the hearing happening,
is the Self; tasted, tasting and smelled, smelling—
all is part of Self.

Then there is the part that is aware
that there is smelling happening, as well as the smell,
and that which is being smelled (when there is)
this is Self. That's the same as what it is
that is aware of seeing happening—
this is the Self too.

Self is all inclusive, being an expression that
is aware of itself, of all that is, in each moment.

Awareness or Infinite Self

This week's invitation is to explore Awareness or Infinite Self. It can be a common mis-take to mix up looking at what happens in life as being "wrong" or "right." As people become more aware in their lives, they start to distinguish when they are moving toward recognition of Self, or not. It is a mistake to say that when one is engaged (lost) in some sort of habit, or engaged in their story, that the story or the habit is not part of Self. I have heard people say: "That's not Self" when they see someone (usually someone else) being engaged in a habit.

"Self" is the same as "Awareness." Every single happening, every form, or that which can be sensed at all in any way, is part of "Self" or is "an expression of Self."

Awareness does not differentiate between how that Self shows up…that means that in the biggest sense, whether one moves consciously toward Self or not, all is Self anyway. To move away from the Self, or against one's own nature, is still part of Self—and this might recur millions of times before the choice to move toward Self is made.

Here with Canela, the only theory that makes any sense is that we go through many lifetimes until we move toward recognition of Self…that we choose to commit to that as the most important aspect of being alive, until the Self meets Self Consciously—that the Truth is Realized. This is when each person realizes the Truth of What Is, not in thinking about it, as an experiencing of Self. All one can "do" is commit 100 percent to move toward that, to the best of one's ability, until it occurs, until it is experienced directly and completely.

These invitations—looking at what it is that is reading right now for instance—point directly to the experience of realizing Self.

So how does one explore this Self? To stop, right now, and check out what it is that is aware that there are words on this page—that Awareness is aware of reading happening, to look to see what that is that is aware of even the question of "what is Self?" ...Right Now...

All of this points to experiencing That which is aware of itself. Not the happenings in it, not the display of Self—be it positive or negative (moving towards its Self, or away from its Self in resistance)—that which is Aware no matter what it is that is happening.

One might see all that is happening and be able to distinguish (in the display of Self before you and in you) that which is moving toward itself and that which is moving away from itself. It does not mean that that which is moving away from its Self is not Self—it is all the Self no matter what.

Awareness/Self is aware without judgment; it is just witnessing "What Is'" witnessing its own Self—a witness that is not outside of that which is being experienced, a witnessing that is part of all that is occurring....no division whatsoever.

Taking Anything Seriously?

This invitation is to look at, and practice, not taking form in formlessness so seriously! So here we are, a conglomeration of molecules dancing as a person reading words. Dancing in what? In space, in the Absolute, form dances itself...this is already happening without thought, without will, it is simply happening. So what's all this seriousness around the drama of one conglomeration, or form, towards another? What's to judge...really?

The next time something feels serious to you, look again. Remember that it is only molecules dancing before you, revealing themselves to you as this form (perhaps a person). Allow yourself to see and feel the moment and its reality; all drama may come to a lovely, silent end. You don't need to take my word for it—explore this invitation and find out for yourself!

It's all about exploring the eternal, silent, ever present part of you and that which is dancing in it. You are invited!

Form in Formlessness

This invitation is to recognize that everything, including yourself, is only form in formlessness. It is an illusion. The only part that is real is the actual experiencing happening. This is "a happening"—not what was experienced or what will be experienced—it is the experiencing itself.

What does that really mean, form in formlessness? That you and all that you sense with your senses, see form as the Universe expresses itself. Apples appear to be in an apple form, scents in the form of however they smell, a mom or a dad appear to be forms, a wall or the floor appear to be solid. Really, you and everything that appears to be in form, are made up of molecules that have more space between them than the space the molecules themselves take up. We are much more of a "gap" than solid matter, this has been proven scientifically and is likely something that you know is true. Allowing yourself to feel into this possibility—that you are not what you appear to be—can be freeing.

As you look at this experiencing, ask yourself...what am I experiencing right now? What if I let go of how things appear to be and relax open to another possibility?

What part of you is looking? What part of you looked for that which is being experienced? Look for that part. Connect with That.

This is all about connecting with That—the eternal part of you. The part that encompasses what appears to be solid; the gaps in between the molecules; and all that Is as well as that which is aware of it all.

Support yourself to connect with That directly, consciously.

You Are a Happening

This week's invitation is to look at, and play around with experiencing yourself as a "Happening." It's true that this is what you are, as far as any "you" in existence…you are a "happening," not a thing.

In an attempt to make sense of our world, we categorize it into "things," when really, there is no "thing"…no-thing.

Take a look at yourself for instance. You are a vibrating mass of molecules, always moving, vibrating. In each and every moment, there is movement, there is change, even if you sit absolutely still, the body's process continues on; the energies that are in conjunction with the system are constantly moving, changing; the mind is perhaps chewing away on itself.… no-thing remains the same. In reality, there is nothing to point to that stays in the same form, it only appears to be. This is the illusion of what appears to be.

This invitation then, is to sit and be still, be with yourself and explore the reality of no-thing…check it out and see for yourself if what is being said in this invitation is true or not.

Fear may rise in response to this possibility that is being offered here. Fear can be a normal human response as some part fears that if you were to let go into this nothingness, you will no longer exist. And this is true, "you" will cease to exist and what remains is this amazing conglomeration of energy that continues to express itself as you in each moment.

Spend some time to feel and experience yourself as nothing at all—as a happening in each moment. Experience the freedom and joy of letting go of the idea of "things" and allow yourself to register the expression, in each moment, of That!

CHAPTER SIXTEEN

Opening to "What Is"

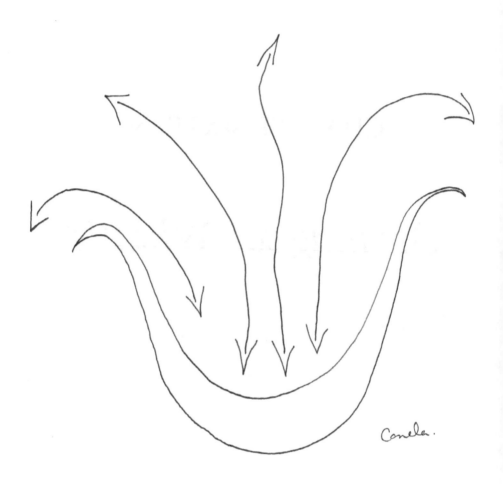

Canela.

"What Is" points to the very moment…
"What is' is not about the past,
that would be "what was."
It is not about the future,
that would be "what will be."

"What is" is always about
right here, right now—
everything that is happening
and the part of you that is
aware of all of the happenings.

"What is" is a very handy little phrase that
you can use to support yourself
to even more presence in your life.
Checking out "what is"
will always bring you
to the present moment: Now.

Pushing or Receiving

This week's invitation is to practice "Receiving"—letting go of "Pushing" in your day-to-day, moment-to-moment happenings.

Instead of pushing yourself to get something done, stop the push, slow down, and move with the moment you are in—receive the moment. It may be simply walking across the floor towards the door, or bending down to look for your shoes—very simple happenings, yet vast in the possibilities of receiving.

Receive (consciously) your breath as you move, receive the felt sense of your muscles moving, your body stretching, feel the blood pumping through your system, your heart beating, relaxing those eye muscles, let what is being seen come into your eyes, feel your feet connect with the floor. Move With yourself, allowing yourself to receive your direct experience. When this occurs, all else will follow more softly, more lovingly…try it out, and feel it for yourself.

Peace and Flow

This week's invitation is to invite a greater level of peace and flow into your life. Stopping and letting yourself register what is happening from an inner perspective, has the side effect of clearing the space around you and bringing yourself into the moment—really, allowing yourself to actually be aware of experiencing the moment. You are, after all, always in the moment; it's just a matter of being aware of that experience...slowing down enough to let your attention Be With That.

Being with yourself (with what is actually occurring) naturally allows a greater level of peace and flow in the movement of life within and without because you are moving With life, with all that is. Dedicate yourself to experiencing That and the strengthening of attention being With each moment...no matter what.

Experiencing "No Mind"

This week's invitation is to let go of any idea of attaining an experience of "No Mind" since, if you look, there is no mind. There are thoughts, or not, and there is either an engagement in them or not, but when you look for it, there is no actual "mind" that you could actually let go of. In some moments, there are no thoughts, just something like empty space, with something simply being aware of that. And this is an experience; often very peaceful when one compares this experience to another experience of lots of thoughts happening with lots of engagement in those thoughts.

Meditation is so supportive a space to see what exactly you have been up to, and then learning to let go and allow whatever is happening without engaging in it...simply being aware of it.

Practice your choice point of engaging in thoughts or letting them just come and go—Being With What Is.

CHAPTER SEVENTEEN

Expansion

Conela.

Expansion is what is happening with this Universe.

*You are part of this Universe so it is
also happening with you too.*

*Knowing this, or being aware of this
supports even more expansion—
it can support you
to relax open to what is happening
when you know that it is simply
the Universe doing its thing.*

*Who are we to get in the way of the
Universe after all?*

Moments and Time

This invitation is one that invites you to slow down in the midst of your happenings and become even more aware of each moment and the movements within that—the side effect is time expansion.

It sounds weird, but it is true—if you slow down and be aware of what is actually happening, moment-to-moment, those moments actually expand and you will have more time.

As each moment becomes more and more full with happenings, as your own awareness expands to encompass more of what is, what appears here as time also expands.

So there is no need to rush. To be timely, really, is a matter of slowing down and allowing awareness to expand. If you stay focussed on where you are attempting to get to, or what you are attempting to get done, time will feel like it is a squeeze.

Meditation is a way of supporting slowing down—turning your attention to what is happening within and without, without moving your body at first. And then eventually also supporting awareness in the midst of movement, so that all happenings become a living, moving meditation.

Application of Attention

This week's invitation is to apply your attention to what works in this world. Your attention is a valuable part of Consciousness, expanding whatever it is your attention is on. If your attention is on "how bad the market is," then you are supporting the market being off. If your attention is on the miracle of a human body, then you are supporting the human body to be even more of the miracle that it is.

Tend to your attention, decide to become more aware of what it is focused on, and consciously put it on happenings which support the greater good—for yourself and this world in which we are all a part. Where attention goes, expansion happens.

This is not about disregarding what is happening; more it is an invitation to let the information which may not be particularly delicious go through you, and to focus instead on the amazing multitude of beauty and love that is all around and within you in each and every moment. Be responsible with your attention.

This is a support for you to be even more responsible with this Gift, the Present, of Being yourSelf. It is a support for you to allow for this shift in Awareness, to deepen That.

Set Your Energy Field for Support

This week you are invited to a little more mastery with what you get to tend to: to set your energy field for support. This setting yourself up for support will diminish any need to spend energy on protecting yourself...after all, it is only an idea that you need to protect yourself at all. If the idea occurs to you to attempt to protect yourself, it is usually too late because if you are aware of whatever it is, it is already with you.

Letting go of spending any energy towards protection supports expansion of you, simply because then that energy is with you at rest, not in resistance to what is.

You can set your field to receive any and all energies that come your way to be supportive to you. For instance, if you happen to think that someone is wishing you ill, there is no need to try to avoid the energy of it, instead you can welcome it as valuable attention toward you and simply allow it to transform as it comes into your field—that no matter what it appears to be to begin with from the apparent other, it becomes transformed into supportive energy for you.

Here are some steps you can take to set your field for support:

1. Sit comfortably with your spine as straight as possible. Close your eyes.

2. Take a deep, long, slow breath in, then exhale long and slow. Take another breath, again long and slow in, long and slow out.

3. While still breathing long and slow, register the weight of the body in the chair; the chair is supporting your body fully. Relax even more into the chair.

4. Allow yourself to feel the form of the body, where clothes or air meet the skin. Breathing long and slow, feel the form of the body.

5. Next, feel or imagine the energy field around this body of yours, breathing long and slow; feel it or imagine it, surrounding the body for the first foot or so. Let your attention rest with this energy field, breathing long and slow, giving yourself time to feel it, to register it, to be aware of it.

6. Although this step is not necessary, it is supportive to imagine white light throughout the energy field, also through the body. Breathing long and slow, feel what happens when the light is with you.

7. Once you are aware of the body, form, and energy field in the felt sense, that you are directly feeling it right now and connected, simply state: "Whatever comes into this field today will be supportive to me." Repeat this twice more. Imagine the words come out of your heart area, radiating outwards and into the field of energy around you.

Repeat this exercise for a few days to get more comfortable with it. Perhaps you may feel to record your voice saying these instructions if you wish.

Whenever you feel you are going to be in a space that you think or imagine is not supportive of you and your heart, like in a courtroom, or an office where you know, or imagine, you are about to deal with people who may not wish you well, take a few moments in your car, or in the bathroom if that is what is available, to do this exercise beforehand. Then open to the energies from all, you can relax open and let them come to you as it is now supportive energy.

In reality, everything is "for" you; all happenings are supportive to you. This exercise can support your confidence to relax open to all that is.

Spending time feeling your body, the form, and the energy field, will strengthen and expand all of it in response to your attention. It is already worth the space/time spent and then, adding your preference, you get to witness what happens in your day, how it can strengthen you in your receiving all that is. It can support confidence in you when you see the effect that you can have when you spend time with yourself...being aware of what is.

Expansion of Whatever You Would Like

This Satsang topic is expansion, with the choice left up to you as to what you would like to expand in your life. Considering that all is Consciousness...yourself, the air, the thoughts, sound...you are invited to celebrate this and simply ask for what you would like—to state your own preference at this time of your life—expansion of That.

Consciousness does not differentiate between what it is in all of its appearances. All is absolutely equal, made of the very same stuff—so how could something be "more" or something "less"? It expands into more of itself with attention—your attention. For instance, stating a preference for a deeper level of honesty with yourself and others—this will enhance and expand honesty in your life...which is one way of supporting one's self toward living in the awakened state. If this is what you want, then commit your attention to it, being willing to go wherever it may lead you.

This is support for you to follow your own way of Being, your own path. Commit to that even more deeply...you are invited!

Afterword

It is my sincere wish that this book, these Invitations, have been supportive to you in some way—more enjoyment, more love, more trust, more peace, and more awareness (any or all of those) about yourself is the purpose of this book. It is why the Invitations have been written.

If you have any questions, or wish to share what has occurred with you in response to anything in this book, please feel free to write to me through the "Contact" page of the website www.canelamichelle.com.

I would love to hear from you!

Sincerely,

Canela Michelle Meyers

About the Author

Canela Michelle Meyers has given herself over to service of humankind. Born a multi-sensitive being, she sees and experiences life as movements of energy in each moment, yet is not removed from human predicaments, challenges, or opportunities.

Canela supports people to relax open to, and experience directly, the Awakened State of Being. Once this has occurred, she then supports people with integration, embodiment, and settling into living life in each moment. Her expertise and skill in supporting herself and others directly, consciously, has come from working with thousands of people (first as a ReiKi Practitioner/Teacher; in Satsang gatherings/sessions; and also in the corporate setting) since 1994.

No matter what the format, greater expansion, acceptance, and awareness is what she enjoys supporting people to allow—making their lives more peaceful, enjoyable, and abundant.

She now resides on Bowen Island, BC in Canada and also in Manzanillo, Mexico, when she is not travelling around the world offering Transformational Satsang gatherings and retreats.

Check out her schedule for more information. To invite Canela Michelle to offer Satsang in your hometown/business or for individual or couple Satsang sessions via Skype, go to: www.canelamichelle.com.

Made in United States
Troutdale, OR
11/21/2023

14786161R00139